the ART *of*
CONSCIOUS
CREATION

the ART *of* CONSCIOUS CREATION

how you can transform the world

JACKIE LAPIN

Published by Elevate, Charleston, South Carolina.
Member of Advantage Media Group.

ELEVATE is a registered trademark and the
Elevate colophon is a trademark of Advantage Media Group, Inc.

Printed in the United States of America

ISBN: 978-1-60194-009-4

Most Advantage Media Group titles are available at special quantity discounts for bulk purchases for sales promotions, premiums, fundraising, and educational use. Special versions or book excerpts can also be created to fit specific needs.

For more information, please write: Special Markets, Advantage Media Group, P.O. Box 272, Charleston, SC 29402 or call 1.866.775.1696.

Library of Congress Cataloging-in-Publication Data
Lapin, Jackie.
  How you can transform the world : the art of conscious creation / by Jackie Lapin.
      p. cm.
  Includes bibliographical references and index.
    ISBN 978-1-60194-009-4 (alk. paper)
  1. Self-actualization (Psychology) 2. Consciousness. 3. Visualization. I. Title.
  BF637.S4L357 2007
  153.3--dc22

                                                                    2007018210

t a b l e   o f   c o n t e n t s

As I write this book I am confident that it will be a best seller because I am Consciously Creating my future. In the past two years I have awakened to my infinite power, my ability to influence the immediate world around me and the world at large. It has been the most exciting journey of my life and has opened a door to a future that inspires and electrifies me.

Electrify may in fact be the most appropriate word because in this book I equate the physics of frequency and wavelength with the power of consciousness. For those of us whose cosmology is one of faith, this embraces the concept of divinity, the powerful force that drives our lives forward. One can equate "The Universe" with God and our "soul" with higher consciousness. But for those who don't believe it is God, then simply see this guidebook as a way to manipulate the physics of frequency to enhance your life and change the world.

The Art of Conscious Creation: How You Can Transform the World is a manual for empowerment. It is a wake-up call for those who have spent their lives feeling powerless, victimized, or buffeted by life's challenges. With the awareness of your infinite powers to create your own reality to change the future, to change the world, you can set an exciting new course as so many others around the globe are also doing. For you are not alone. You must have felt it — a growing sense of urgency drawing people toward a new awareness or a higher consciousness; a greater inner desire for a rich spiritual life; a need to **do** something to fix a skewed world. Millions around the globe are having this same awakening and are asking: "What can I do?"

Each of us can learn the skills and the art of Conscious Creation. First apply your skills close to home and then join with others in very specific acts of vision to co-create this new world — a world of peace and abundance, dominated by love, honor and respect. If you are skeptical, I only suggest you apply the techniques in this book consistently for a few months and see if they transform your life as they have mine.

My background is probably much like yours. I'm just trying to make a living and have a little fun. I've spent the last thirty years as a pioneer. Initially as one of America's first women sportswriters, and then building two very successful businesses — the first as a leading professional in the field of media relations and publicity and the second selling mineral spheres and natural mineral marbles (round rocks) on the Internet to collectors and hobbyists worldwide.

I have come to believe that every entrepreneur is a visionary, and that we use the tools of Conscious Creation to manifest the businesses we create in our minds. I think that is true for most successful people. Take for instance the comments of actress/singer and former Miss America, Vanessa Williams, as she told *Parade Magazine* recently: "You have to have fire. You have to have a dream and some kind of drive and vision to propel you on."[1] Now how's this for vision: Taylor Knox, champion surfer and the first winner of the Big Wave Challenge that annually honors the surfer conquering the largest wave, told his parents as a third grader that he was going to become a pro surfer. Then in the sixth grade he wrote in a class assignment that he wanted to grow up to be a pro surfer *sponsored by Channel Islands Surfboards*. Guess what? He did. Like Taylor, I told my parents as an eleven-year-old I would grow up to be a sportswriter. At age twenty I was a writer at the Detroit Free Press; at twenty-one I was at the Associated Press and at twenty-two I was at the Washington Post. I was a Conscious Creator before I even knew it!

Once I segued into the media relations business, my vision helped to manifest effective publicity campaigns for my clients and an abundant life for myself. I noticed, though, something very significant along the way. Whenever money was in short supply, when I worried about paying my staff or the rent, the money would just appear at the 11th hour — just as long as I made moral choices and lived by a code that I felt was in keeping with Universal ethics and principles. I began to trust the Universe would fulfill my needs, and that I was embraced by a power that appreciated my integrity. It appeared to be looking after my well-being.

Indeed I feel blessed, but each of us looks at our lives and sees the shortcomings. So I then embarked on a quest in my 50s to see why I wasn't as happy as I'd like to be and what I could do about it. With the guidance of many people more wise and in touch with the Universe than myself, I began a personal transformation that has led to planting the seeds for a global transformation. Sage writers like Wayne Dyer, Louise L. Hay, Carolyn Myss, Shakti Gawain, Esther and Jerry Hicks and many others provided vast amounts of knowledge. I had long felt that my skills were meant for a much bigger forum. While mentoring young people throughout my career and using my talents as a publicist on a vast scale (helping to initiate the worldwide poker boom, for example) were meaningful activities, I was created for a larger purpose. So using the skills I had acquired for meditating and asking the Universe for answers, I queried, "What is indeed my purpose?" The answer came in a sudden flash with an electrical charge — an incredibly powerful resonance in my body — like I have never felt before. The vision for this book and for teaching world transformation using Conscious Creation was laid out in a vision before my eyes. The moment of profound connection with the Universe, when I felt like I was one with the Universal power, has set me on this course.

While I write, I have instituted Conscious Creation to my life in the most intrinsic way — on little matters and big transactions. What I desire just seems to come my way. I wanted an inexpensive black pearl bracelet to match the ring I bought in Tahiti. I put it out to the Universe. It was staring at me from a jewelry store window a week later. I wanted an extra day this week to work on this book even though it looked jammed with media relations work. I set forth my vision and a day opened. I had been having trouble with insomnia. So I set my intention to sleep solidly from the moment I put my head on the pillow until the alarm rang. For the first time in months, I began having a full, restful night of sleep. I set my financial goals for this year, sent them into the Universe. I will make them with dollars to spare. When I am concerned about possible friction at a meeting, I cast out my net of peace, calm and love — and the meeting turns out to be fantastic. This power of Conscious Creation — of control — is exhilarating! Certainly, not everything is within my control. But by making subtle, but powerful shifts, I set my future going in the direction that I choose it to go — not that is chosen for me by seemingly random forces. As I enact the power of Conscious Creation by raising my frequency so that it meshes with the Universal energy, my life becomes easier, happier, more fulfilling and more inspired.

Because I come from the "secular" world, I see myself as the link between the wonders of mastering the Universal energy and the everyday person. You don't have to be a mind/body/spirit guru to become a "person of the light." As we all awaken to the infinite power that comes from the interface with our own energy and that of the Universe, we are creating a whole new species of conscious people resonating at an amazing level of influence.

My role is to be a tuning fork, calling each of your electromagnetic energies forth, tuning them to a higher pitch, and focusing that unified wave on creating a better world for all of us. It is within our reach. We just have to envision it!

In peace, serenity, joy, love, surrender, trust and acceptance,
Jackie Lapin

ENERGY:

The CURRENT *of the* UNIVERSE
WHAT WE THINK *is* WHAT WE CREATE

I magine an Earth in the throes of peace! People of every culture and race respect each other, help each other, and work together for the good of humans, animals and the environment. In this world everyone has enough to eat, adequate shelter, work that is fulfilling and sustaining. The global economy is balanced and everyone is reaping the benefits. Science is working to protect our treasured planet and heal all of the illnesses that have scourged the globe. Businesses are **adding** benefits and vacation time for workers, while executives and shareholders are sacrificing their profits just a bit in order to ensure they are bringing to market the best quality products **and** making the right moral choices. Worldwide and national leaders are truly "men and women of the people," working for the benefit of their constituency, not the strengthening of their own power base. Global warming is a thing of the past, solved through worldwide corporate and government cooperation. Alternative fuel solutions are in use everywhere. Everyone practices energy and resource conservation. People of all ages are kind and polite to each other, thoughtful and considerate. Everyone feels safe at home, the office, and when traveling since crime and terrorism have dwindled away.

Clearly this is not the world we live in today.

It could be!

Our world today is a world we and our ancestors created, a world that has been driven by our most primitive fear — fear of being controlled by others; fear of not having enough land, food, money, power; fear of not being good enough; fear of failure; fear of not being loved or not being lovable. We feared and so we projected fear. Our thoughts became our reality.

That is because our thoughts and our emotions are more than just ideas and momentary feelings. They are *energy*. They are vibrations that we cast out into the world...either loving and kind, benevolent high-vibration frequencies that create a safe, prosperous, loving, munificent world; or they are fear-driven, angry, self-hating low frequencies that poison ourselves, our loved ones and friends, and the Earth.

For just as we humans are living organisms that absorb and emit energy, so is the planet on which we live. As we continue to bombard our world with energies that are rife with fear, jealousy, resentment, anger, guilt and self-denial, the Earth becomes the energetic repository. Like a bank, it takes on our deposits. If we feed it healthy, loving, compassionate energy in the same or greater measure, we'll all be experiencing a very different reality.

Here's a quick look at where mankind's negative thinking has gotten him today. These snapshots represent more than man's action, they also represent the debris of his fears and emotions.

- More category 5 hurricanes than ever charted in history

- The most deadly tsunami ever chronicled

- Record floods

- Terrible droughts causing the destruction of forests, the drying up of reservoirs, the huge loss of wildlife, widespread crop loss and starvation everywhere from the western U.S. to the Sudan and Ethiopia

- Record-setting wildfires around the globe

- Polar ice shelves breaking away and melting in days instead of eons

- Nearly 1,000 animals on the Endangered Species List are considered "threatened"

- The outbreak of AIDS, Bird Flu and a variety of primitive microbes and viruses that have yet to reveal their destructive power

This is just the natural side of the balance sheet. Now let's look at the human side:

- Wars, insurgencies, genocides in Iraq, Sudan and the Middle East

- Threatening powers with emerging nuclear capabilities in North Korea and Iran

- Corporate pirates lying, cheating and stealing from their workforce, their customers, their shareholders and the taxpayer

- Governments choosing to spend money on warfare instead of healthcare; on pork-barrel subsidies instead of alternative fuel sources or housing

- Terrorists, anti-Semites and racists perpetrating their hatred through violence, death and vituperation

- Poverty, crime, drugs, lack of jobs, and poor schools driving the cycle of perpetual misery in cities around the world

- Obesity reaching epidemic proportions in children and adults

- Heart ailments and cancer continuing to overwhelm the medical system, despite huge advancements on the treatment side

- Autism and ADD-learning disabilities becoming pandemic

- Everyone seems to be on anti-depressants

- The very scientific methods that medicine relies on for safety and effective health solutions corrupted by special interests

- Young people coming out of colleges having less earning power, higher housing costs and less job security than the preceding two generations

- People are curt with each other, children cast away parents to gain their inheritance, drivers are fueled with road rage and kids are so ill-disciplined they disturb everyone in a restaurant or other public place

○ Pedophilia, domestic abuse and other forms of violence against women and children are on a dramatic rise

Are you angry and feeling powerless yet? Well, don't be, because you can help change your world. You are, in fact, one of the most powerful beings on the planet.

With every emotion we feel, we send out energy that either contributes to the construction or destruction of the peaceful world that most of us would like to enjoy. You don't have to be either the corporate raider or the abusive husband. You just might be a man who feels guilty for not spending more time with his children or the woman who hates the figure she sees in the mirror because it carries a few extra pounds. Those energies log into the global "bank." On the contrary, when you feel good because you have reached out to a stranger, taught someone to read, kissed your elderly grandmother, exercised your body or selflessly helped a co-worker stuck on a project, you've put healthy, high-frequency vibrations into the "bank."

FOR WHAT WE THINK AND FEEL IS WHAT WE CREATE.

As you will learn in the chapter on "How the Universe Works," what we focus on, we manifest and attract. If we turn our attention to envisioning the world in which we want to live, through time, effort and shared vision, we can begin to mold and shape it to that image. It is through our vision, the tool of our imagination, that we emit the energies that transform. Through the harnessing of joyful imaging, creating loving mind pictures of a kinder world, we transform and replace the negative, low-frequency energies that have dominated the past. This is because high-frequency energies are far more powerful than the opposite. These energies resonate with the Universe's desire to give mankind the peace and contentment it desires.

So why have we come to this place of worldwide desperation? It is because we have relegated our creative visionary power to people who are consciously or unconsciously driven by fear. Fear is the most potent kind of global pollution. What we believe — consciously or subconsciously — determines how we perceive the world and, more importantly, the world itself.

It is time we cleanse ourselves of fear and take back the power. We are the ultimate creators. It is time we remember who we are and why we are here. Try manifesting in your own life first, using the techniques we suggest in this book. Then step back. Don't be surprised when your desire arrives in some form or another. Think about how many times before you've wished for something that came to pass. Your desires, your emotions and the positive energies you emitted manifest your wish. (You manifested it because, on some level, you believed you could.)

We can do the same with the world around us by using conscious creativity — envisioning the world we want, making it real in our minds and hearts before it becomes real in the physical plane. There is no need to feel foolish or powerless thinking that you are just one person. Each one of us is an enormously powerful being for transformation. It only takes one person to ignite change in the world or inspire others.

Anthropologist Margaret Mead understood this when she said: "Never doubt that a small group of thoughtful committed citizens can change the world. Indeed, it's the only thing that ever has."

But you will no longer be just one, or even a few. We are approaching a spiritual crossroads on this planet, where millions of people are realizing there must be something more, something better. They are awakening to a call for spiritual self-responsibility and global cleansing. It is a summons for us to evolve to a higher consciousness of being. It's time to learn we are one with the Universe and we have the power to create our own reality, both personally and as a consensus reality. As you begin your visions for personal and global transformation, others will match your high-frequency energies and desires. Like a tuning fork resonating with other vibrations on the same frequency, this united vision will be unlike any force ever before. It is a remarkable synergistic power that will be life changing for all of us.

See it, feel it, so be it.

TIME TO TURN THIS AROUND?

Here are some stunning facts that point to the impact on our planet of negative energy and unconscious thinking. In recent years there has been a considerable increase in severity of natural disasters and international health calamities. Our world is waiting for us to awaken and turn away from the brink of disaster. We have our work cut out for us. However, if we start Consciously Creating and committing ourselves to action now, success will be ours! There is no time to waste.

- According to the Weather Channel, in 2005 the Atlantic Basin saw the most Category 5 hurricanes ever charted in one year. There were a record 28 storms, of which 15 were hurricanes, exceeding the 1969 record of 12 hurricanes, and 7 were major hurricanes. Katrina was the costliest and deadliest hurricane to ever strike the U.S.

- The most deadly tsunami ever chronicled struck in December 2004 with more than 300,000 dead, 1.7 million displaced.

- We are now seeing record floods, including the one that killed 54,700 in North Korea in 2006

- The National Interagency Fire Center says that 2005 broke the wildfire record in the U.S. with more than 8.7 million acres burned. While the total number of fires was down, the acreage burned was way up. 2006 is on record to exceed the previous year-old high.

- The U.S. experienced the hottest summer on record in 2006 according to information from the National Climatic Data Center.

- The National Center for Atmospheric Research claims the world will face far more deadly heat waves, intense rainstorms and prolonged dry spells before 2099.

- The drought gripping the American West could be the biggest in 500 years with effects in the Colorado River basin considerably worse than during the Dust Bowl years, according to scientists at the U.S. Geological Survey. The report said the drought has produced the lowest flow on record in the Colorado River. According to the Los Angeles Times, in 2006 the American West was in the eighth year of its most severe drought since record keeping began in 1895.

- A report commissioned by the British Government issued in October 2006 said that without substantial spending global warming will reduce worldwide productivity on the scale of the Great Depression, devastate food sources, cause widespread deaths and create hundreds of millions of refugees.

- According to the Natural Resources Defense Council, the Ward Hunt Ice Shelf had been around for 3,000 years before it started cracking in 2000. Within two years it had split all the way through and is now breaking into pieces. Images from NASA satellites show the area of permanent ice cover on the Arctic polar ice cap is contracting at a rate of nine percent each decade. If this trend continues, summers in the Arctic could become ice-free by the end of the century. Since 1979, the size of the summer polar ice cap has shrunk more than 20 percent.

- Rising temperatures are already affecting Alaska, where the spruce bark beetle is breeding faster in the warmer weather. These pests now sneak in an extra generation each year. From 1993 to 2003, they chewed up 3.4 million acres of Alaskan forest, states the Natural Resources Defense Council.

- Scientists project as much as a three-foot sea-level rise by 2100. According to a 2001 U.S. Environmental Protection Agency study, this increase would inundate some 22,400 square miles of land along the Atlantic and Gulf coasts of the United States, primarily in Louisiana, Texas, Florida and North Carolina.

- A study by scientists published in the journal Science in November 2006 says all of the world's edible fish will be gone by 2048. In 50 years 90% of the world stocks of tuna, cod and other fish will have vanished.

- On the Endangered Species List there are 988 species, 276 more are threatened, and 58% of the species have gone extinct since the list began. The Sierra Club says the average length of time species recovery plans take to be effective is 30 to 50 years.

- More than 650 gray whales have washed up sick or dead on the West Coast of the United States in the first five years of the decade; 75% of the kelp forests of Southern California have disappeared; 97% of the staghorn and elkhorn coral have died off the Florida coast since 1975; 14,000 seals, sea lions and dolphins arrived on the California shoreline sick or dead between 1995 and 2005; 200,000 of the 500,000 albatross born each year die within days, mostly from eating human trash; 150 oxygen depleted dead-zones have been identified in the oceans around the world. (National Oceanic and Atmospheric Administration, Nature, Virginia Institute of Marine Science, California Department of Fish and Game, Los Angeles Times).

° The National Foundation for Infectious Diseases cited these areas as their top 10 concerns: Antimicrobial Resistance; Bioterrorism; Emerging Infectious Diseases; Gastrointestinal, Diarrheal and Food-borne Diseases; Hepatitis; HIV and AIDS; Hospital Acquired and Opportunistic Infections; Sexually Transmitted Diseases; Tuberculosis, Vaccine Preventable Diseases (including flu).

° New diseases with potential to become pandemic: SARs, Avian flu, and a variety of microbes under observation.

° The Institute of Medicine maintains 20% of children in America will be obese by 2010.

° Since 1981, more than 25 million have died from AIDS and amFAR estimated 40 million currently are living with HIV or AIDs worldwide, 2.2 million of those are children under the age of 15.

chapter two

WHAT'S LOVE GOT *to* DO WITH IT? EVERYTHING!

There is one vibration in the Universe that is more powerful than any other. It is the transcendent quality of love, the highest frequency energy that exists.

It's not just the love of a person for his or her spouse, or a parent for a child. It is love of life, nature, humanity, self, and self-creativity. It is the passion we bring to our work, play, homes and our deeds. It's in how we interact with others that we are given the opportunity to express love.

Furthermore, love is catching! Have you ever noticed what happens when someone walks into a room with a smile? Love — and all of its derivatives: kindness, compassion, consideration, joy — has a ripple effect. I remember seeing a friend of mine graciously offer money to a hungry person outside of a supermarket. Until then, I had never given money to a street person, but I looked at his kindness and I wanted to be more like him. I decided I wanted to be kinder and so I set my intention to be more compassionate. His act set my new standard of behavior. I am now quite good friends with our local bag lady and regularly make "deposits" of money and my time with her. Mostly, she just likes someone acknowledging she is a valued member of humanity. Members of my family, however, also reaped the benefits. I just took time to be a nicer and more thoughtful person. It was the beginning of my awakening.

We can all learn from my friend. Love is our E-ticket to the new world.

From an energetic standpoint love is the vibration that resonates with the Universal life force that drives the cosmos. Fear is what happens when one is cut off from that force. Have you ever been with someone you just knew was "evil?" That's because that person's low-frequency energy had strayed far from the source. At every moment of life, we are given a choice between love or fear, connection or disconnection from Source.

Loving emotions, acts and thoughts put us in unity with this great power of the Universe and all of its creatures — large, small, human and otherwise. Because each of us is one part of a giant whole, living a high-frequency life smoothes the ride since we are vibrating at the highest energy level, connecting with the Universal Intelligence and resonating on the same wave. Want an easier and more fulfilling life? *Surf the love vibration.*

Whenever we act, we have a choice to create our new reality. Do we take the path that makes us feel good, kind, considerate, moral, forgiving — thus emitting high-frequency energy? Or do we take the "easy" way — lying, manipulating, bullying, moral equivocation? In the latter case you may have an exultant moment, but the residual feeling won't be one that would make you proud. Further, you'll be contributing to the accumulation of negative vibrations that feeds a world of strife and unhappiness. Let's not forget that since "what goes around comes around," there will be other consequences directly impacting you. Karma is one example of a perfect and consistent energetic law of the Universe. In these particular times its action works in an accelerated fashion.

So let's see how this "energy thing" works in practice. Because I'm a Type A personality, I am someone who often responds with anger when thwarted by bureaucrats and store clerks. As I became more conscious in my visioning, I decided to test the theory. I had a patio umbrella that just fell to pieces after being in the sun for a few months. Now, I no longer had the receipt and it had been five months since the purchase. Under normal circumstances the store, a leading home improvement retailer, would never have taken it back. So I put my mind to enveloping the department manager, someone I had yet to meet, with love and kindness, and envisioning him taking it back with grace. Then, I picked up the phone, called the store and explained my predicament, asking for his help. Here is what the manager said, "Under normal circumstances I wouldn't take this back. We'd have you return this to the manufacturer. But you know what, we'll just make an exception and take this back. We'll give you store credit whenever you come in." That was it. Since I didn't come in with an "attitude" and instead projected onto him my positive energy, envisioning the end result, I got exactly what I wanted...my desired intention.

I tried it again a week later with a difficult client, one that others had alerted me was roiling for a fight. So before meeting him, I mentally bathed myself in the symbolic pink light of love and then threw a net over him as well. I pictured the interaction going well. When we met, he was nice as could be and the meeting went off perfectly.

Then there was my relationship with my neighbors. For years I had been asking them to eliminate the brush in their backyard. They kept asking me to cut my trees so they could have a better view. Things weren't headed in a positive direction. So instead I envisioned a happy resolution, and that's exactly what I got. I cut a few trees, and they landscaped their yard asking me all the while about my preferences in the areas that were visible from my house. Now we get along great!

Try it yourself. It really is magic!

So if this magical use of conscious visualization and projection of love can work so well on an individual level, just consider its power of transformation on a worldwide level.

I think it is very well summed up by Barbara Marciniak, author of *Path of Empowerment*: "In all its many splendors, the exultation of love is the ability to see the point, purpose and significance of life's events, to willingly transcend and release old, worn out patterns of perceptions and belief and lock them into place. Once you come to a true understanding of the power of love, you can safely venture into the areas of both physical and non-physical reality in need of cleansing and healing."[2]

HOW *the* UNIVERSE WORKS

W e all have free will. But here are certain Guiding Principles that determine how our conscious and unconscious choices reverberate back on us and impact the greater world. These Principles are the core operating guidelines in the Art of Conscious Creation and Global Transformation. Just like you have a MAC or a Windows Operating System determining precisely what you can do with your computer before you can create your document, the Universe has a code or operating system which defines the way things work. Master these principles and you can begin to manifest much of what you can conceive.

I call these Universal Guiding Principles, rather than "rules" or "laws" because I perceive the Universal Force to be a benevolent, loving, energetic power, not authoritarian or vengeful. These guidelines are like the ropes of a children's playpen. They are given to us to bounce off, ponder our experience, learn and get back into the game again with new insight. We're here to learn, evolve, expand and find a path that brings individual passion and joy, as well as global contribution.

Whether you think of this guiding force as energy, the Universe, or God — it's running the show! No doubt you've experienced many of these principles in going about your daily life — some in a good way and others you'd rather soon forget. Yet the idea is not to forget, but to learn from such experiences. For, they — and the Universal Guiding Principles enabling those experiences — hold the key to allowing you to live the life you want and manifesting the world you desire.

As you learn from them, reflect on how you have contributed to the reality that you are living, and what changes you can affect to empower the future. While each of these principles operates on a personal level, they are equally powerful on a global level. In fact, since all are connected, personal experiences also affect global ones. As Mahatma Gandhi said, "Be the change that you want to see in the world."

UNIVERSAL GUIDING PRINCIPLE 1:
Everything is Energy: The Power of Vibration

On a certain level it's very humbling to think that this incredible thinking engine that we are is really just a mass of unseen little atoms and molecules mostly interspersed with space, gyrating to various frequencies otherwise known as energy. On a higher level, it is tremendously empowering, as energy is not burdened with the limitations of physical existence. Science tells us that we are electromagnetic beings, and we take this as truth, even though we don't see it with our eyes. Furthermore, science informs us that everything we touch, feel and see is also made of tiny atoms doing the same energy dance, sending off vibrations. Because such matter emits low energy vibrations we can see it, but the faster it vibrates, the more likely we cannot see it. Think X-rays, infrared rays, ultraviolet light, radio waves, etc. Yet, you can begin to sense our power and our relationship to the universe. Realize that science — the New Physics — has also shown these vibrations take the form of either waves of energy OR particles of energy, totally depending on whether a human being observes them or not!

Everything in the Universe has its own distinctive vibration or frequency. As spiritual and physical humans we are energetic beings, careening around the planet, sending and receiving energy. Even when we sleep or are not conscious of interacting with the world, we are transmitters, putting our own energy imprint on others, the globe, our future. Just like the physical aspect of ourselves, our thoughts and emotions also create energy transmissions. That energy interacts with other energies. Before you know it, you've changed or created something new. We'll address the science of this in greater depth in the next chapter.

Our life force, *chi, prana,* odic force, inner light — whatever you choose to call it — is an energy that pulsates through us and animates us. The world is slowly awakening to the miraculous flow of this energy and how it impacts our physical health, or mental state, our emotional blockages and our spiritual interface with the Universe. This is the energy harnessed and directed in martial arts, yoga, transcendental meditation and many other Eastern philosophies. With the explosion of alternative healthcare in the world today (acupuncture, acupressure or healing touch, chiropractic energy work, cranial/sacral and various forms of holistic health applications that are gaining favor), it is easy to see that both patients and practitioners are becoming aware of how our unseen energies can be the key to healing our bodies, hearts and souls. Even insurance companies have come to recognize the effectiveness and value of some of these modalities by covering their costs.

While most of us today cannot see the energy that humans emit, there are a growing number of people walking the planet today who can and do see it as a very real phenomenon. These people clearly see energy emissions as *auras.* The colors of the emissions and the direction of energy flow they perceive can tell them if you are angry, happy, sick, peaceful or confused. Each of the seven main *"chakras"* — or energy vortexes — in the body emits specific messages that contain information about free flowing energy or blockages. Such blockages contribute to our unhappiness and ill-health, since these *chakras* are also repositories of memories — thoughts in energy form — that can inhibit health. Clearing them can return someone to health quickly and completely. Science is just now beginning to corroborate the existence of the *chakras* and this energy system that is such a powerful part of our being.

Interestingly, more people see these energies than want to admit for fear of being discredited or thought insane by the world at large. Some, however, are coming forth now as the Western world is becoming more tolerant of such phenomena. What was the fringe is now becoming mainstream. But it doesn't take someone with a gift for seeing auras to sense another person's energy or vibration. We all do it when we encounter someone new or walk into a room and get a "sense" of the atmosphere. That is your "receiver" opening up to intercept the others' energy — individually or collectively — and to read its vibration. Someone's face only tells part of the story. If you think back you can probably remember a time when someone smiled at you, but you knew that was not their true underlying emotion. Maybe that person gave off a "tell" as they call it in poker — a physical or verbal giveaway — but most likely you just had a "gut" feeling. The *chakra* located in your gut or solar plexus region was doing its job of informing you.

When you are in the presence of someone who loves or cares for you, there is a warmth, a peacefulness, a feeling of comfort. That is because the person is emitting high vibration energy directed toward you. When there is anger or tension, you're being bombarded with low-frequency emissions, an unpleasant feeling at best.

What drives the Universal dynamic is this scale of frequencies. Thoughts, emotions, actions operating at the top of the scale are love and all of its expressions: kindness, compassion, forgiveness and gratitude. These frequencies are closest to the loving and joyful vibrational nature of the Universe. It's the heritage that we have been bequeathed, if we can only recognize that in vibrating at the same frequency of the Universe, we draw to ourselves its munificence. When we are in this state, we feel most "alive." Have you ever noticed how you feel in nature? Most people feel vibrant and present because they are in direct contact with the naturally high vibration of plants, trees, minerals and water. The sun is a primary and powerful source of great positive energy as its sunlight rains on you. The higher we personally vibrate, the closer we are to an authentic alignment with the Universal life force, the Oneness, that opens the door for tranquility, self-fulfillment and global peace.

Correspondingly, the bottom of the scale is driven by the expressions of fear, hatred, anger, jealously, guilt and blame. We see the results of this everywhere — in wars, genocides, corporate greed, marital infidelity on a grand scale, and much more. Lower frequency energies reflect a separation from the Universal force, someone who has lost his way, whose spirit has become disconnected from the goodness and harmony manifested in the Source.

There is more than just a sense of well-being that is available to us at the higher frequency levels. There is wisdom, information and guidance. For it is on those higher frequency waves that our "intuition" hops aboard. You need to know if the job you are weighing is in your highest good? Ask the question, ask for signs, and then listen and watch. You'll have an answer. It may be a "gut" feeling, or a friend who suddenly calls with some information about the company, or a message that you hear in a song. Much of the time, though, it comes if you are quiet, turn your thoughts inward and wait for an answer. By living in alignment with the Universe, staying in the higher frequencies of emotions and thoughts, we open the channel between us and the Universal Intelligence. We have access to unlimited knowledge, guidance and truth that enrich our higher selves, as well as our terrestrial selves. In fact, our very existence and experience as human beings — our terrestrial selves — serves the greater existence of our higher selves. Thus, we can tap into the Universal knowledge bank at will.

It is also through high vibration visioning, creating and acting we manifest our desires. Prayer, when enlisted on behalf of a beneficial cause, is a form of high vibration energy. According to Esther and Jerry Hicks in their insightful book *Ask and It is Given:* "A good feeling emotion indicates vibrational alignment between the perspective of your Inner Being and you. A bad-feeling emotion indicates vibrational misalignment between your Inner Being and you. You must ask yourself: 'Is this belief vibrationally compatible with my desire?' Because if not, you cannot achieve your desire…You will discover that it is not difficult to find and activate your beliefs that harmonize with your desires, and when you do, your intended desires will become your manifested reality."[1]

Global Implication

What this ultimately means is that we are enormously powerful creatures, wielding a potent tool for the betterment of the world and ourselves. It's in learning to harness our energy — to manage it — that we can transform our lives and transform the world on a small scale or a large scale. It's a big responsibility — this Conscious Creation. It is also a magnificent gift. But the alternative is UnConscious Creation, which is exactly what we have. If you don't recognize how your thoughts and emotions impact your life or the world at large, then you are bound to spew out more negative energy that perpetuates the status quo. More importantly, by choosing to "live in the light," emitting good vibrations, you will have a powerful counter energy to the hatred and negativity dumped into the Universe by the unenlightened. Being aware of one's choice to control his or her own frequency is the beginning of what is called "Consciousness." So here is our chance to take the reins and create the life we want and the world we deserve.

UNIVERSAL GUIDING PRINCIPLE 2:
Everything is Inter-Connected; We Are All One

We have seen how personal energy is a primal force in the world, but why and how far-reaching is our power? One answer is we are all links on a giant daisy chain. Everything is inter-connected because we emanate from the same source. We are one part of the giant whole. Think of us as one trans- former on the Universal energy grid. Remember when small transformers caused massive blackouts in California and the East? *Little* things can have *big* ramifications. Maybe you think your acts, words, deeds and thoughts only impact your immediate world. But have you ever thought about the person who took your words to heart, using them to interact with the next person and so on? Each of us in some way operates like bumper cars on a global framework.

Just think, though: if we are all one, if we each bear a share of this Universal life force, then every human being is more than just a member of our species. He or she is a part of us. This has profound implications on how we should treat each other. It means that in judging others and finding them unworthy, beneath us, ordinary, or contemptuous — we are judging, disrespecting and disavowing a part of ourselves. The realization of this for me personally made me stop in my tracks. It made me examine my thoughts and now I oftentimes consciously take them back. Today, when I find my- self discounting someone, I say to myself, "This person is doing the best he or she can. Have patience and some understanding." I try to look for their gift, whatever it may be — their contribution. I make myself listen, instead of quickly turning away to get back to what I was doing. Also, I try to send a little love their way, just as a member of the human race. The act of reconnecting with humanity, respecting the dignity of all living creatures for that matter, is an act of love that resonates far and wide in the fabric of the physical and non-physical planes.

Much of the world's discomfort and misery comes from feeling disconnected from each other and from the Universe, though that might not be a conscious realization. This "disconnection" is an illusion, because there is no way to truly become unplugged from the Universal grid. We can tune it out (become Unconscious) or grow very distant (live within the low-frequency range) but we are still part of the Universal mass consciousness.

Says New Age sage Shakti Gawain in her book *Path to Transformation*: "Whatever attitudes and beliefs are held most deeply and powerfully in the mass consciousness will, for better or worse, be manifested in the collective reality... Our own thoughts, feelings, and actions are not isolated occurrences taking place within the confines of our own bodies, but are in fact manifestations of the one spiritual and energetic source that moves through every one of us. It is no more possible for one of us to change without changing the rest, as it is for a single wave to crest in the ocean without affecting the whole."[2]

Global Implication

So here's the truly great news about interconnectedness:

1. *There are no Lone Rangers.* No person is ever really alone. The Universe is there to support you and the rest of its citizens. Just reach out and envision the embrace of all you wish to be on your support team. Hold them in your heart. You are calling them to come to your aid. You are calling the Universe to help you reconnect with the forces that make you whole.

2. *Powerful You!* One person, one thought, one action can have a profound effect. Consider Thomas Paine, who wrote the Revolutionary War pamphlet *Common Sense,* which caused the patriots to stand behind their demand for freedom; or Mahatma Gandhi, whose non-violent movement gained India its independence from Britain;

or Martin Luther King and Rosa Parks whose acts of civil disobedience, courage and inspiring oration drove the Civil Rights Movement. But it doesn't have to be on such a grand scale. Millions of people whose names and faces have never appeared in a newspaper are changing the world. It began with their visions, carried into action, and became part of the mass consciousness. They are transformative people — just as you can be and are becoming.

3. *You are Everywhere!* Your energetic power is not limited to humanity. It reverberates in the entire seen and unseen world. Plants, animals, the atmosphere, the land, the sea, our weather will all benefit through the uplifting energy and vision that people — individually and collectively — work to manifest. The entire planet is a living intelligence impacted by the vibrations that it absorbs.

4. *The More the Merrier!* By uniting with others, the power of shared vision can be magnified a hundred times and more. The energy of tens, hundreds, or even thousands, vibrating to the same frequency — followed by some form of action — will speed up enormously the global transformation by making a significant impact in the mass consciousness. *Yes, there is a happy and peaceful world waiting!*

Our most curative healing powers are activated when we reach out to embrace the power of the Universe. We conduct the charge through us as if we were simply a lightning rod for Earth, grounding the goodness and implanting it in our reality. By setting in motion an intention, energized by the power of our hearts and the belief in its success, we can reverse years of global misery and damage — all by consciously knocking over that first domino.

UNIVERSAL GUIDING PRINCIPLE 3:
Transmutation of Energy

We each have a very special gift that makes us the primary transformative agent for change in the world. It is the magical ability to transmute negative energy to positive energy, to bring light into the darkness.

A Universal guiding principle holds that high-frequency energy transforms low-frequency energy. An example is the power of love or true forgiveness can disarm, dismantle and wipe away the residue of hate. This is the energetic equivalent of "turning the other cheek." By replacing resentment with acceptance, self-hate with self-love, guilt with compassion, the negative energy loses its power and gives way. In science this is demonstrated by the entraining of a less powerful frequency — say a sound wave — by a more powerful one. This enables us to compare the spiritual world with the physical one: "As above, so below." Many of history's compassionate religious and secular leaders have known this secret and gone into the world to teach it.

There are numerous stories of people faced with an attacker intent on violence, who met their attacker's rage with compassion and calm. Anticipating fear or resistance instead, the attacker is disarmed by this unexpected empathy, and walks away, leaving the person unharmed.

Drawing in the high-frequency of Source can create seeming "miracles," transformations of healings that defy what is perceived to be "normal" expectations. Cures that are totally unexplainable by traditional means are recorded all the time now. Some of these are credited with being extraordinary examples of "mind over matter." An excellent guidebook on creating the "miracle mindedness" that fosters these remarkable transformations is *Let Go: Let Miracles Happen*, by Kathy Corboda.

High ideals — be they the yearning for freedom, a desire to raise up the populace, a quest for economic independence — have enabled countries in modern times to manifest peaceful revolutions. By choosing the peaceful protest over violence, they succeeded in birthing new nations. Consider the peaceful revolutions of the Ukraine, Georgia, the Czechoslovakian states, The Philippines and the new Russia.

Fear is what keeps the world "stuck" in its unhealthy spiral. People's basic desire is for love and its manifestations: acceptance, respect, safety and financial security. The fear of being without any of these drives the fear that taints the world. Meeting fear with love, understanding, empathy and consideration is a powerful and unexpected message, and has the ability to defuse fear, change thinking and take the anger out of any confrontation.

Next time you are in a confrontational situation, try a little empathy. Let the other person understand that you care about his or her viewpoint and that you value his or her input. See it through his eyes. Gently ask how the two of you might work out a compromise that would be in everyone's benefit. Don't defend your position. Throw out a mental "net" of peace and love around the two of you. Speak from high-vibration energy, the charity of your soul, a position of mutual welfare. Remember how in reality the two of you are connected.

There are other simple ways to adapt this amazing transformational custom in your life. Look past the negatives in others. Acknowledge their gifts. See the good in any situation. Hold the belief that from negative situations come positive ones. Be the person offering the glass half full, not half empty. These are transformational beliefs and behaviors. Once you put this practice into your daily life, your family, co-workers, friends and business associates will notice a difference.

Letting go of negative feelings and energies directed to the outer world, however, is only half the picture. You must apply the same transformation to your inner self. When you feel darkness overwhelming your soul, when rage threatens to overtake you, when feeling afraid, guilty or sad, you have the power to transform these energies with their opposites. Give yourself the same magical makeover. Embrace good thoughts about yourself and the world around you. Forgiveness, compassion and gratitude are great starting points. Be the best friend to yourself that you would be to someone else. Imagine living the joyful life you desire. Light illuminates darkness. You are the light. Light can travel across universes.

Global Implication

Millions joining together creating visions driven by high-vibration energy will wake up the world. Indeed, we have already started to do so. Such unified action will attract others to the purpose. From these waves of high energy visions, thoughts, emotions and actions that blanket the world and its inhabitants, we can diffuse, dissipate and transform negative energy, negative actions, negative policies, negative beliefs that keep the world in a stranglehold. It may not be an overnight change, but change will come and faster than we might presently imagine. It may not be exactly as we individually envision, because ours is a consensus reality. But whatever change transpires will be for the highest good of mankind. Like candlelight marches of committed people walking hand in hand, we can keep coming forward, showing the way. Remember that one flame can light endless others.

UNIVERSAL GUIDING PRINCIPLE 4:
I Love Myself, I Love Myself, I Love Myself!

Remember that old adage "God Helps Those Who Help Themselves?" Nothing could be truer as well in the energetic sense. We have two supreme relationships when we come onto this planet. The first is with The Universe. The second is with ourselves.

These relationships are perfect and whole in the beginning, but the perfect relationship with ourselves begins to deteriorate almost from the moment we arrive. Negative thinking and emotions undermine it. The problem begins in childhood when someone tells us we aren't pretty, we aren't good enough or we're not smart enough. Whether that's parents, peers, teachers or others who imprint the message, those painful feelings and emotions get deeply buried. They become part of the belief system about who we are. Furthermore, they tend to dictate how we interact with the world and how we treat ourselves.

Here is how human nature responds to this bombardment of unconscious negative energy. A person either recedes or overcompensates. A woman told she's not beautiful either hides her light from the world or becomes obsessed with her appearance, weight and image. A man told by his father that he is worthless or stupid either fulfills his father's image by never realizing his highest abilities, or he sets out to prove his worth to his dad by becoming obsessed with wealth and achievement. Neither strategy brings peace, harmony and joy to their lives. It just leaves the big painful wound untouched or makes it bigger.

Self-hatred is the big wild card in the global consciousness deck. Few of us on Earth today have surmounted this obstacle without tremendous serious effort, whether that is through therapy, self-help books, meditation or the counsel of friends. Almost everyone carries a shadow of varying degrees from this powerful character killer. In its extreme people seek drugs to drown out the voices in their head that reaffirm their unworthiness. For most of us, though, we bumble along, not liking what we see in the mirror or sabotaging our lives in small or large ways. We pour out lots of negative energy into the world along the way.

However, global transformation is as much about changing the world as changing ourselves. We have to start with us. By clearing our own negative beliefs and emotions and replacing them with self-love and compassion, we in turn open the door for the Universe to transform our lives. We can then invite the guidance, wisdom and good fortune that we deserve, but just don't know it yet. The Universe thinks we're perfect and totally worthy! We just have to get it through our own heads and hearts.

So here are some simple rituals that when practiced regularly can begin to open your heart to yourself. You can't do them "half-heartedly." You must tell yourself you believe these things, and then, as they say in therapy, "Act As If It Were True" and you believed it.

- Stand in front of the mirror every day and say: "I Love Myself, I Love Myself, I Love Myself."

- Remember that you are part of the perfection of the Universe. If you believe in God, you are part of God, so you must love who you are.

- Begin making lists of all your attributes ... Really think about what makes you special.

- Tell the Universe how grateful you are for your attributes and the gifts you receive.

- Think about your words. Change any thoughts in your head or words about to come out of your mouth diminishing you.

- Focus on the image of your perfect self. Then imagine yourself that perfect self. Tell yourself that you are that perfect self.

- Ask friends and family what they love about you. Write these down and stick them on your mirror.

- Every night when you go to bed, ask the Universe to bring you the peace of self-love and self-respect.

- Meditate. Go inside yourself and sweep out any negative thoughts and beliefs that keep you in the animated suspension of self-loathing. Envision a little broom or paintbrush sweeping them away.

○   Do physical exercise that makes you feel good in your head and your body. Anchor this feeling. Tell it to transform the other feelings.

○   Treat yourself like you are worthy, whatever you do. You are your own best friend. How would you treat your best friend?

○   Forgive yourself for whatever you did or felt; it's in the past. Your unblemished and happy future is ahead. Make each day count.

○   Start your day every day in the shower or tub with a healthy round of self congratulations and self love. Tell yourself what you will do that day to feel good about yourself. Water imparts high-frequency energy. You are doubling your high-frequency transformational capacity.

Affirmations

Affirmations are statements you make to yourself and the Universe that proclaim your readiness to receive. They are short phrases that say in a positive way what it is you wish to attract to your life and what you are becoming. They express a belief that you can truly experience what you are expressing. You can create an affirmation for everything you seek to achieve. For example:

1.   I am a beautiful, happy, self-realized individual who embraces my own uniqueness.

2.   I am deserving of total abundance and now embrace its arrival.

3.   I have everything I need in my life now for total happiness.

4.   I am releasing all fear of success and manifesting the perfect job.

5.   I am now attracting a loving, satisfying relationship with a partner into my life.

6.   The Universe is guiding me and I embrace its wisdom and protection.

Such affirmations help with the process of personal transformation and the clearing of negative thinking that blocks goodwill from coming our way.

Each of us has a person of unlimited potential and joy hidden inside. We just have to let it out. Clearing negative energies, washing those *chakras* clean of negative messages and memories is a life liberating experience. A little unconditional love goes a long way!

Global Implications

The gift of unconditional self-love we give ourselves is the same medicine we need for healing the world, it's just on a smaller scale. We become much more powerful creatures when we practice healing from a body and soul that has no obstructions, which can simply conduct and re-direct the Universe's miraculous power of unconditional love.

On an interpersonal level, relationships are often undercut or sabotaged by a person's need for approval from his or her partner. This is a result of insecurity, self-doubt or self-hatred that is present. A healthy relationship consists of two people who not only love each other, but love themselves. This takes the "neediness" or "desperation" out of the equation. A good relationship between two loving partners has many implications for the world:

- Emitting unconditional love times two in the world

- Better, happier and more fulfilled children who contribute to a balanced world

- Happier more self-realized people in the workplace

- People who are less fixated on themselves and more on serving others

UNIVERSAL GUIDING PRINCIPLE 5:
The Universe is Knocking. Open the Door!

The Universe is a pretty nice place to live. It really wants to give you everything you desire!

The Universe is naturally benevolent, since it runs on a fuel of unconditional love. It wants us to share in that energy and to realize all of those dreams we hold dearest. Our birthright is harmony, happiness and goodwill.

So let's stop messing this up and join the party!

The Universe lands us on Earth as natural, happy, little creatures and then, we as humans, proceed to seal ourselves up with layers of misery and unhappiness. If we want to "get back to the garden" as Crosby, Stills and Nash once said, we need to unpeel those layers.

We each have infinite potential for complete joy, happiness and fulfillment. We were not put on this earth to be unhappy.

Here are some steps to take that clear the way for goodwill to come straight on through:

1. ***Think positive thoughts!*** Cleanse yourselves of fear, let go of worry, make moral decisions, and trust the Universe to see that you get what is in your highest good. Give and accept unconditional love. Stop allowing your brain to run rampant with negative fears about the future and negative self-talk about yourself. In choosing to turn off this unproductive aspect of your mind, you can redirect to positive thoughts that inspire and attract goodwill. Remember happy moments. Love *this* moment. Be grateful for this day and for what joys are in your life. Right away you've increased your vibration of joy that resonates with the Universe and says you're readying yourself for more joy.

2. ***Let go of control, or fearing your lack of it.*** (This has always been one of my biggest hurdles!) If you trust in a benevolent Universe, than you don't need control. Everything will come out right. Now when I make myself crazy, I sit back and say, "I'm just the co-pilot here. The Universe is the pilot." It's dizzyingly freeing! We waste enormous amounts of energy in trying to gain or maintain control, when we can simply surrender to a Universe that's looking after us anyway.

3. ***Become the co-creator of your own Universe.*** Envision your life as you want it to be, feeling yourself living that life, enjoying the wonderment of that life, then being grateful for it having been given to you (even though it hasn't arrived yet.) (More on this later.) Start with little requests. You can work your way up to the big ones.

Then open the door. Don't be impatient. That's a form of resistance, which is a negative blocker. Create with no expectation of what exactly will come or when or how. Detach emotionally from the ultimate outcome. Just have a quiet confidence that whatever arrives will be in your highest good and continue to emit happy, high-frequency energy. Surprises await!

Global Implications

There is a better world out there waiting. The Universe is anxious for us humans to get with the program. When we can tip the balance of energy-enlightened people — "people of the light" — over those who are living in darkness, the Universe is ready to download us a world of goodness.

UNIVERSAL GUIDING PRINCIPLE 6:
The Universal Magnet: Get Ready! Here it Comes!

Remember when I said we are electromagnetic beings? This leads us to a very elemental principle that is essential for all of us to grasp: *What we think and feel, we attract.* It's a simple phenomenon of energy. High-frequency attracts high-frequency and low-frequency attracts low-frequency.

A wonderful sage named Lynn Grabhorn said in her book *Excuse Me Your Life is Waiting*: "Whatever we're feeling is what we're vibrating, and whatever we're vibrating is what we're attracting."[3]

If you are vibrating fear, victimization, and hopelessness, you'll attract more negative energies. This is how some people become perpetual "losers" and "victims." On the other hand, if you vibrate joy, happiness and love, wham! It's coming to you. That's why positive thinking people (glass half full/optimists) tend to attract success and negative thinking people (glass half empty/pessimists) get exactly what they fear is coming to them. This is a true self-fulfilling prophecy.

This "law of attraction," as it's called in the energetic world, is all about where we put our focus. If someone dwells on a wrong that was done to them, more bad things will begin lining up in their future. If you focus on a "lack" of money or time, the universe will send you just that — a **lack**. If you focus on abundance, prepare to head toward the bank.

I saw this happen in my own media relations business. Though I knew this principle, I just couldn't seem to unlock my focus from dwelling on a projected shortfall in the company billing for the three months ahead. So suddenly, contracts I thought might come in began to disappear, one after another. I finally got a grip on myself, doing a lot of meditative work on my mind and my first-through-third *chakras*, the ones that deal with earthly matters of money and security. I let go and handed it over to the Universe. At last, the fear disappeared. The next day the calls began coming in. I ended up with twelve new business calls in four weeks, half of which became clients.

The message to be learned is to *focus on what you DO want, not what you DON'T want.* When we focus on what we want, the universe will support us in securing those results.

This includes the kind of people we attract into our circle. A person emitting high-frequency energy will find other like-minded individuals coming into his or her life. Some old low-frequency individuals may even fall away, or you may choose to let them go because they drain your energy. If you are focusing with joy and an expectation of success on a new project at work, you'll attract the right high-minded people to help you complete the project.

If you find low-frequency people hanging on, try to be helpful and kind, but don't allow their negative wavelength to interfere with your high-frequency energy. In fact, you have the potential to become the agent of change for that person's transformation if you can get their awareness — remember high-frequency can trump low-frequency.

This principle can be put to work in a group setting, too. As a high-frequency individual coming into a group situation, you can join with and motivate a core group of high-energy individuals. As a unit you can help move this organization forward in a positive and product manner. The group may then reach out to embrace the low-frequency people and help them to rise to a higher vision.

When we feel strongly about something, this is an important checkpoint. It's a reminder to take an inventory as to what energy you are emitting. You need to become aware of your feelings and thoughts and make corrections before you begin engaging that Universal magnet. However, if you find yourself dwelling on the negative, the good news is that negative thoughts need not have long lasting ramifications if replaced with positive thoughts and feelings. The Universe can change course in an instant.

Global Implications

On a grand scale this clearly is one of the reasons the world is in such a mess. Each time there is tit-for-tat violence in the Middle East, one can see the fallacy of the "Eye for an Eye," principle. When you are violent, you attract violence. When you seek to oppress, you are oppressed. It happens in the energetic world of intention and then is manifested in the world of reality.

However, if we allow the sadness, sorrow, misery, horror and disappointment to well up in us because of the day's headlines, it takes away our power to act in a way that counters this global "dis-ease." We have to protect our energetic core, and this means monitoring how much violence we see on TV and the movies, how much angry dialogue we listen to on talk radio, how much unpleasantness we read about in newspapers and in books. As you begin to go down this path, you may find yourself eschewing violent films and thrillers, and shoot-'em-up dramas on TV as I have. I also limit the amount of local news I watch on TV. While we all need to be aware, we cannot dwell on these matters daily — and thus attract negative energies to us. It's a fine line we walk: caring and wanting to take action in the world without taking on the negative energies ourselves. We have to stay focused on the good in the world and how we can contribute to it.

I admire how Marianne Williamson chose to view the unfolding 2006 outbreak of war between Israel and Lebanon. Instead of dwelling on the tragic escalation, she issued this powerful message on her blog: "What the world needs now is a miracle, and it is miracles to which we are all entitled. For miracles occur naturally as expressions of love; they are in fact the natural order of the world when the mind is in its natural state. Our task, quite simply, is to love in a way that we have never loved before. Let us love even those with whom we do not agree, perhaps even those whom we might think we hate. Let us love them not personally, of course, but impersonally. Let us reach for the Love of God within us, that we might reach the Love of God within them. Let us all awaken to a higher truth, that we might be subconscious awakeners.

Neither Israel nor Lebanon need any of us to fall into this nightmare with them. What they need is for us to remain spiritually awake — to the truth of their Oneness in the Mind of God. Because all minds are joined, our being awake will help them all to awaken. Their souls are making an ultimate sacrifice for each of us, showing what lies ahead for the world should we not remember who we truly are."[4]

We can stay centered through positive thoughts and deeds, no matter what is happening around us and continue trying to attract for the world and ourselves a better future.

UNIVERSAL GUIDING PRINCIPLE 7:
What We Think is What We Create

Thus far, we've mostly talked in generalities about negative and positive frequency energy and how we can apply this to our lives and the world at large. But here's the part where we begin to learn about the *Magic!*

What we envision, we can create.

Let's set an intention: Do you want a better car? Believe you are worthy or deserving of it. Hold in your vision the car you want. Feel yourself driving in it. Feel the joy of having it and loving it. Spend a lot of time on this joy part because emotion is what emits the vibration. Then say thanks to the Universe for bringing it to you. Do this regularly for a month. Then let it go. Forget about it. Leave it in the Universe's hands. Unless you've blocked this some other way with negative backwash, there's a pretty fair chance that it may just become reality. Maybe not on your timetable, but when the Universe deems you ready to receive it.

Got a problem with a co-worker? Envision you working together happily, getting along great and turning out terrific work. Throw that "love net" over him or her. Experience in your mind the fun and joy of working together and seeing eye-to-eye. Say thanks to the Universe for bringing about this great improvement in your working relationship. Take one step to improve the situation. Then give it to the Universe to fix.

Want to manifest your true love? Write down on paper the qualities of the person you want to come into your life and what you want in the relationship. Don't forget to write what you intend to bring to this relationship, too. Then envision this person coming to you and being with you. Think of all the things you will do together. Experience the joy of being in a relationship surrounded by unconditional love. Be in this feeling! Then say thanks to the Universe for bringing you your soul mate. Go out and do one thing that might bring you closer to your intended — join a dating service, sign up for a special interest club, go to a co-ed gym. Just the act of doing **something** signals the Universe you are willing to take the first step. Then let it go into the ether — with love.

This is the Art of Conscious Creation, when we chose to attract specific energies or desires to us. What we think, we can manifest.

This also works on the opposite principle, however, by being unconscious of what we manifest. We may draw things to us that are not what we think we desire. It may be what we need (because the Universe often fills a vacuum with a painful lesson), but it may be what we **allowed** to happen. This is UnConscious Creation.

We can take charge of our reality by Consciously Creating much of what we want to transpire in our lives or inviting in what we want to possess (if your desire doesn't cross the line into greed!) As we become conscious of our thoughts, emotions and deeds, we can begin to take stock of how we've manifested the life we have now. Changing one's attitude, goals or self-vision can change a person's personal reality, as well as the global reality. (Remember that everything is interconnected.) Says Wayne Dyer, in his best seller *The Power of Intention*: "Change the way you look at things, and the things you look at will change."[5]

Awareness opens the door for change. It empowers you to take charge of your life. This is the "law of attraction" put to work on your behalf. Decide what you want to bring in and then attract it. No thought is neutral. It has the power to attract, to manifest. This is an awesome responsibility. It forces you to acknowledge that yours is the life you've created. But it also gives you unlimited ability to create the world you **DO** want.

The higher the frequency and emotion, the faster it manifests. Thus joy, happiness, love, and desire to serve others put you in a vibration that will attract your desire much more quickly. That's because your passion super-charges the delivery. Have you ever noticed that when you are doing something about which you are passionate, something that gives you great happiness or satisfaction, other good things suddenly come your way or help you reach your goal? You're "magnetizing" yourself for Universal goodwill.

This works especially well if you hold the Universe is a benevolent force, just waiting to hear what's on your wish list, something like Santa Claus waiting to hear who's naughty and nice. The "nice" part really greases the wheels. If you want to know why you should make the effort to become a positive person or to rethink how you are living your life, here's a very good reason. You'll unblock the chimney.

Conscious Creation is about learning to master our mental, emotional and spiritual messages. If we want better direction and greater control over our lives and future, we have to take personal responsibility for the thoughts we put out into the Universe. We have to change our beliefs to be consistent with what we want to attract. Says energy healer Barbara Brennan in her book *Hands of Light*: "We perceive the world in ways consistent with our expectations, beliefs, and past experiences. Thus we create our own experiences."[6]

What's truly exciting for anyone who embraces Conscious Creation is the awesome opportunity that this presents. No longer are you at the mercy of "fate" or "others" or "the past." You have the ability to start fresh and redesign your future. It's like being offered the chance to do a complete makeover on your house by one of those reality TV shows! Only it is a makeover on your life. This doesn't mean that everything will change tomorrow. What it does mean is that you have clarity on what you want, signaled the Universe that this is your intent and put the wheels in motion. Eventually, things will begin shifting in your direction.

Two cautions here:

○   Just be careful that what you ask for is in your highest good and in the Universal highest good.

43

° Be very clear on what you want. No doubt you've heard folks say, "Be careful what you ask for; you might get it." Unclear or unspecific messages can turn up some interesting results!

Global Implications

The world we have today is a function of a mixture of Conscious and Unconscious Creation by its millions of inhabitants now and throughout the past. In ignorance of its own great power, humanity allows the violent, the greedy and the powermongers to dominate the Universal creative forces — whether those perpetrators are aware of their energetic influence or not. Mankind has given power to the "dark side" by default. With growing awareness in our own Conscious Creativity, we have the ability to begin taking it back. By holding a higher vision in our hearts and minds, controlling and directing the energies we have at hand with some positive action, we can supersede the "dark side." Our intentions are our values. Let the better values become a light unto the world.

UNIVERSAL GUIDING PRINCIPLE 8:
What We Say is More Than Just Words

To this point we have explored the energetic power of thought and feeling. However, words may indeed have the most potent impact, because they create immediate consequences in the physical world. Add to what you are now learning about thoughts and feelings carrying an energetic charge, you won't be surprised to find that words do as well.

Certainly, how you choose to express yourself will determine what action or emotion will be forthcoming from the listening parties. Condescension, anger and annoyance will undoubtedly have a negative impact on BOTH parties, since the recipient will not be happy and will likely lash out, fail to be cooperative or simply recede into an emotional shell. Undoubtedly, it won't achieve whatever was your original intent. Better to stop and think, "How can I phrase this to recognize this person's dignity and at the same time get him or her to willingly change position, do what I desire, or help me with this task?"

How we treat each other must become a focal point of the new world we want to create. If we cannot treat our neighbors, co-workers, the clerk at the store, even strangers we meet with a high degree of civility, we will undermine our vision. Words are the front lines of civility. Loving, kind, compassionate, thoughtful words create like actions and have far-reaching consequences.

We must monitor our words because those words become currency in the Universal energetic system. What you SAY is also what you manifest. So if you lie to someone, that lie will come back to you. If you speak truthfully (kindly and diplomatically!), that truth will stand in your favor.

This principal also works in our everyday lives. If you say, "I'm working hard to get this done…" –the Universe will make you **work hard**. If you say, "I'm not very good at this…" –you will surely not be very good at it. If you say, "I blame the government," — than expect a visit from the IRS. If you say, "I hope this will happen," — you've left the door wide open for it NOT to happen. Idle chatter is anything but.

Choose your words carefully. Use words that convey a positive, upbeat message, that are specific to what you want the Universe to manifest for you. And do it kindly.

You *can*, however, re-open the barn door after the cow is out! It's OK to correct your words after they are out of your mouth. Increasingly, I find myself saying, "Oops . . . that's not what I meant," and then restating my comment. For example when I say, "I hope that will happen," I correct myself. What I really meant is "I am confident the Universe is bringing this to me." The Universe will recognize, and act on, the last intention, ignoring the previous one.

The power of words cannot be minimized. They are the messengers of your true self, the most concrete way that we can impact our lives daily and the people around us. Conscious word choice allows us to manifest our reality on a daily basis and mold our future.

Global Implications

When applied consistently, the power of the word to bring people together and diffuse anger is ten times more powerful than the power to incite. As our leaders shed their provincialism and begin to realize that cooperation is our true heritage — and not warfare or divisiveness — it will be their words that open the door for global peace. But this responsibility does not lay solely with the people in power. Everyone can make a stand for peace with his or her words. Words of peace resonate on every level. Every movement began with one person who shared his words with others. The right words at the right time before the right people can begin a global wave that can change the world. We just have to make sure that those words reflect the power of Universal love.

UNIVERSAL GUIDING PRINCIPLE 9:
Abundance Awaits

We have now learned a little bit about ways to manifest abundance in our lives. But did you know that Universal abundance is UNLIMITED!

The great fallacy in mankind's belief today is there is limited abundance on this globe. If I have something, than it means someone else must have less. If I believe that, I have to ensure that I get mine because there isn't enough to go around. This is a false premise.

There is enough food, enough money, enough housing...if we manifest it together. If we stop supporting the "poverty consciousness," we can secure what we desire as individuals and bring forth improved living conditions for everyone else on the planet.

This does not mean that people living a comfortable lifestyle will have to reduce their standard of living. For the average person greater abundance is within reach. It might, however, mean that people who make huge amounts of money will need to be more conscious of sharing it with the underprivileged, creating new work opportunities for others, or taking less so their companies are not strangling the working man and woman on the rungs of the ladder beneath them. No one really needs hundreds of millions of dollars to live comfortably! Consciousness means knowing when your abundance can do more good in someone else's hands.

Unlimited abundance is a function of the belief that we can call forth anything we desire if we envision it, support the vision with action, eliminate the negative energy roadblocks and truly believe that we are worthy and entitled to it.

People who feel financially fortunate, who are grateful for what they have and anticipate their own solid financial future attract more abundance. It's all about their relationship to money and to the Universe. These individuals have an abiding trust the Universe will provide — and it will! They are attracting more money to themselves.

People who fear they can't "have it all," "don't deserve it," "can't handle it," or that money is somehow unsavory — will keep it from coming forth. Individuals who believe that money is the source of their happiness will never have enough, and therefore drive it away. There is also nothing incongruous about having material wealth and spiritual riches at the same time. The Universe wants you to have both of them and live abundantly on both planes.

So how does one manifest more money and success in his or her life?

1. *Give.* The Universe works in checks and balances. The more you give away, the more it will come back to you. But it has to be given freely and not in an expectation of receipt. Helping others will have a direct or indirect benefit to the giver.

2. *Think Positively/Send Positive Energy.* Set your dreams and expect them to be manifested in some way, but on the timeline only the Universe knows.

3. *Be Joyful and Happy*. Abundance flows from happiness. The happier and more upbeat you are, the more you will attract wealth and other forms of abundance.

4. *Trust.* Trust the Universe to bring you what is in your highest good.

5. *Live Morally*. Make moral choices to ensure your channel is open and not blocked by negative energies and negative consequences.

6. *Have Patience.* The Universe knows when to reward your efforts, faith and vision. If it hasn't come, then you have more lessons to learn.

7. *Ask.* Ask the Universe what more you need to know to attract your good fortune. There may be an unconscious block that inhibits your abundance magnet from functioning at its peak.

8. *Don't Sacrifice.* Sacrifice is incompatible with abundance. Know that you don't have to sacrifice to attract abundance to your life.

9. *Believe.* Support the belief in abundance for everyone else and never be jealous of others. Be happy for their success. Know yours will come in time.

10. *Enjoy What You Do Have.* The less you enjoy what you have, the less will be granted.

11. *Be Grateful.* Nothing invites goodwill better than being grateful for what one already has, or what one is going to receive in the future.

It's important to note the principle of unlimited abundance is about more than just money. It can be time, space, freedom, children, joy, love! Whatever you want more of can be called forth if it is in your highest good. Therefore, if you want more time for yourself, commit yourself to volunteering for others. People will come forth to help take the load off of you in other parts of your life. If you love more without strings attached, you'll see a watershed of love in your own life.

Global Implications

Believing there is not enough wealth to go around will create the phenomenon of fear. Raising the income level of people around the world generates economic stability, minimizes crime, eliminates hunger, raises the level of education, fosters economic independence for those living on government support or family subsistence, inhibits disease and promotes health, advances the protection of the environment and has numerous other benefits to the entire family of man. If, as a species, we loosen our grip on fear, we can set a path that will float everyone's boat.

The panic of fear can be seen whenever the stock market goes into a spiral. Individuals who are convinced that a downfall is inevitable watch for the signs then suddenly pull their money out. This causes a general panic — a Bear Market — and the economy nosedives. It's mass consciousness working on a very defined scale.

Changing our beliefs intentionally one at a time to eliminate such "poverty consciousness" thinking will have an invigorating effect on the whole. If you catch yourself feeling competitive for money, work, attention, love — stop and think. If there is enough for all of us in the Universal storage bin then why is there any need to compete? Work **with** your colleagues, companions, family to create abundance for all — not *against* them. Speak up! Help your employer find more ways to make everyone more successful. Join with your community to find ways to raise the standard of living for others. Teach the principle of abundance to those who are mired in the belief they are losers or to people who think they are entitled or somehow more deserving than their neighbors. Every human has a right to happiness, fulfillment and abundance and that right is not to be had at the expense of others.

When we can begin to instill this principle in our worldwide leaders, then we will begin to see real change. Each country can achieve abundance without sacrificing the abundance of other nations, each ethnic group can achieve abundance without taking from others within its nation's borders, people of all faiths can live a good life if they are willing to wish the same on their brethren of other faiths. Belief forces cooperation. For one to succeed, all must succeed. Working to raise the economy in Mexico stems the flow of illegal workers in the United States. Increasing the market and the price paid for sustainable food crops in Afghanistan decreases the drug trade. In turn, many nations' healthcare expenditures and the spiraling cost of crime fighting and pursuing criminal justice is impacted. Giving people work with decent wages and educating them to seek better paying work for the most part takes away the root source of many of the world's ills. If we can manifest better leaders or transform those now at the top to adhere to this vision of unlimited abundance for all as a central tenet of their governments or organizations, we can begin to create abundance. This is the real power of globalization.

FREQUENCY YARDSTICK

Each thought or emotion has a positive or negative charge. Positive thoughts and emotions raise your frequency level, helping you to vibrate in concert with the Universe. The higher the frequency that you resonate, the easier life becomes, the more joy and love you experience, the more Universal knowledge and wisdom are accessible to you and the more powerful you are as a Conscious Creator. As you monitor your thoughts remember they are within your control! Think positive!

POSITIVE	NEGATIVE
Love	Fear
Joy	Anger
Passion	Jealousy/Envy
Compassion	Pessimism
Kindness	Impatience
Thoughtfulness	Frustration
Generosity	Disappointment
Courage	Doubt
Forgiveness	Worry
Patience	Blame
Acceptance	Revenge
Understanding	Insecurity
Graciousness	Guilt
Gratitude	Despair
Respectfulness	Judgment
Peacefulness	Victimization
Trustfulness	Dishonesty
Hopefulness	Selfishness
Optimism	Miserliness
Powerfulness	Ingratitude
Honor	Intolerance
Integrity	Hatred
Honesty	Disrespectfulness
Sincerity	Sorrow
	Shame
	Powerlessness
	Prejudice

UNIVERSAL GUIDING PRINCIPLE 10:
What Goes Around Comes Around

In today's world we act frequently without thinking about the consequences of those actions. Whether that is because of expediency, self-interest, economics, or just thoughtlessness, we often put in motion unintended forces that swing back and take their toll on us, as well as others. No doubt you've experienced this phenomenon, seen it happen to others or heard the phrases "What goes around comes around," "what you reap, you sow" and "Karma." What these all imply is that everything happens for a reason, no action stands alone without setting in movement a chain of events. This is the principle of cause and effect. This is stated very succinctly by Dr. Norman Milanovich and Dr. Shirley McCune in their book *The Light Shall Set You Free*: "Every cause creates an effect and every effect has its origin in a cause."[7]

Indeed, this is a basic energetic principle of the Universe. By unconsciously creating we are nevertheless creating. Imagine an ecosystem. The energy each person feeds into the closed ecosystem has to go somewhere, and while it may bounce off others and careen around corners, at some point it will come back to the sender… perhaps changed in form, perhaps from an unexpected direction — but it will come back. As vast as it is, the Universal ecosystem operates by a very defined mechanism.

Thus, there is a very simple formula for ensuring that you receive back the blessings of the Universe:

1. *Think before you act.* What is the long-term intention — living a good life, creating prosperity for your family, having personal contentment? What is the short-term intention and how does that impact the long-term intention? What action is in concert with both?

2. *Treat others as you would treat yourself — or better!* The basic Biblical Golden Rule is a practical way to apply the law of cause and effect.

3. *Send out only positive energy and that energy will eventually return.* Monitor your thoughts, feelings and actions. Choose those that will manifest a win-win for all. Release the fear that may cause you to make a poor judgment.

4. *Act with integrity, consistency, courage and honor.* These provide lots of credit in the Universal savings bank. They pay off big time! Forgiveness also ranks right up there on the top of the list of deposits.

5. *Be graceful under fire.* Resist the reflex of just reacting. Think clearly and carefully first. The Universe will ultimately give you the time needed to make the RIGHT decision and support you in doing so.

6. *Watch for the boomerang.* Don't be oblivious to the world's interconnectedness. Use negative experiences as a way to think back on your actions to see how you could have handled something better. The incidences may not have had any obvious connection, but the Universe is trying to educate you...to make you sensitive to the power of thought and action.

7. *If you have put something in motion that you regret, ask yourself: "How can I correct this act in some way?"* Is there another act of redemption that redeems the first one? A new action can have the effect of mitigating the first one. And remember to proceed with the consciousness of forgiveness for self and others.

There are times when I respond with a short temper and realize afterwards that I have hurt someone's feelings or diminished them in some way. While it will not erase my hurtful words, I try to step back and apologize. I'll also pay a compliment or offer to do something to lighten their load. I see immediate positive feedback and know that I've begun to repair the damage. Acknowledging my own culpability begins the process of self-forgiveness, which in itself is a positively-charged energy. I know I'm on the right track when the memory of it keeps me from being unpleasant the next time I'm faced with a similar situation. Thank goodness we are all "trainable."

With a little forethought, we can pave our own way with positive energy and actions. Projecting ahead to the eventual likely outcome, making choices that support positive Universal energy dispersion and envisioning a beneficial result for all involved, we'll find our own lives more fulfilling, less stressful and easier. So go out there and create your Karma positively and consciously!

Global Implications

While we all see and feel the impact from the world's governing bodies', terrorist's and religious leaders' actions, keep in mind the motion of continuous rebalancing. Prevent priests from marrying and the church ends up paying millions in settlements to people who were molested by men of the cloth. Oppress the Shiites and the Sunni's become victims in a civil war. Force the people of Eastern Europe to bow to the Communist flag and eventually you will have revolution — peaceful or otherwise — resulting in the rebirth of nations based on their cultural and ethnic underpinnings. Tolerate corruption or take graft as a government official, and eventually the system will turn on you. Advocate family values and then get caught e-mailing teenage Congressional pages with sexual overtures and watch your career come to an end. Our world is an end product of men and women making wrong choices — now and in the past — who had a better choice and did not make it. You always have a choice and it is always between love or fear.

The future can be very different if we can bring consciousness to the future leaders of the world. And make them see the long-term value in making the RIGHT choices, consistent with tolerance, peace, acceptance, cooperation and love, freedom and dignity for all humanity. It's not only a wise move for them as individuals, but for their children, constituency and this planet.

UNIVERSAL GUIDING PRINCIPLE 11:
Moving Into The Light

The unhappiness that many of us experience with our lives and the world around us has much to do with what goes on in our heads — not necessarily what's going on in the physical world. It is centered in our belief system — how we view ourselves and the world around us, self-talk ourselves into various forms of insanity and misery, create illness by not releasing painful memories. We live in pain and want — knowing there must be something better. There is. Each of us can break the habit of pain, let go of the struggle and emerge into the light.

Let's look at some of the key dynamics:

Beliefs

From our earliest childhood, our parents and other adults instill in us beliefs in our potential, as well as our limitations. Each time we are told "no," we learn that we are no longer living in a world of complete freedom to do as we please. We begin to form internal messages from these teachings. As teachers, parents and peers interact with us, we further internalize their perceptions — I'm ugly, not a good student, bad at sports, have poor social skills, too fat, etc. These beliefs drive our ambitions, determine the type of partners we attract, undermine our success. Most of the time we are unaware that such beliefs are prime motivators in our lives. We just think that's just the way life is. Truthfully, our negative beliefs are holding us hostage!

Self-Talk

Inside of us are actually two voices — the voice of our spirit, the one connected to the Universe through our heart; and the voice of our intellect/ego, the one that is solely terrestrial (of the physical world) and is wrapped up in our beliefs. While the intellectual voice is the handy tool that helps us function in the world, do our work, read, play and watch TV, it is also the means through which our ego and beliefs talk to us. That voice is seldom quiet, chattering away, worrying about the future, dwelling in the past, nagging us, re-enforcing all of our shortcomings. It's very much like constant static on the radio (those of us who remember the days before MP3 players.) Who needs this bombardment? Try not thinking for a while. The habit is hard to break.

Health

Those painful memories that we endure and absorb throughout our lives actually lodge themselves in the energy centers and organs of our bodies, disrupting the healthy flow of energy. If humans processed their emotions immediately, releasing their feelings by talking them out, acting on them in a constructive way or just letting them go, we would be a very physically and mentally healthy species. Instead, those pent-up emotions get "stuck" in our energy system. It is an energy blockage in the system that causes disease and ill health. Patients often report to doctors or energy healers that during treatment they undergo a profound and overwhelming re-experience of a memory that provides instant relief and clears it out of their system. The corresponding physical symptom is gone — along with the painful emotion. Numerous excellent books such as Dr. Carolyn Myss' *Anatomy of the Spirit,* Louise L Hays' *How You Can Heal Your Life* and Gary Zukov's *The Heart of the Soul* provide insight into the connection between the spirit, the mind, the emotions and the body. These three books in particular offer guidance on what message the body is trying to tell its owner through illness...what emotion needs to be healed in order to heal the physical body.

Moving into the Light

Becoming a happier human initially takes a lot of effort. But remember what the television commercial says: "I'm worth it!"

Emerging into the light pays enormous dividends on a spiritual, mental and physical level. Consciously taking control over your life begins with the intent to do so.

First, you need to take an inventory of your beliefs. What do you really believe about yourself and your relationship to the world?

I've struggled with my weight my whole life. So here is a list of "false" beliefs I realized I held about food:

- ° Once I break the diet that day, what's the use...I might as well eat anything.

- ° I have no control over sugar, chocolate and other foods I desire.

- ° I can't control my eating when I leave the house to go out to dinner or to travel.

- ° I have to starve to keep my weight off.

- ° I am a compulsive person...there is no in between...I can't eat moderately. It's starvation or splurge.

- ° I can't fit in the exercise because of my workload.

- ° I can't control my eating if I'm not exercising.

- ° Once I start, I can't stop.

- Once I get going eating snack foods, I can't stop.

- When I go out, I can't diet.

- I have no willpower to prevent myself from eating what I desire.

- I can't diet/lose weight unless I have no or little pressure/stress weighing on me.

- I just can't resist the call of something yummy.

- I feel compelled to eat when I feel stressed or emotional.

- I eat to make my inner child feel good and give the adult limited moments of joy when I feel depressed.

- I don't believe I can ever achieve and stick to my goal weight, convinced I will bounce back up again. It's a self-fulfilling prophecy.

- I must have something sweet in the evening after dinner/before bed.

Does this sound familiar to you? Perhaps weight isn't one of your core issues. What is? You may be very surprised about what you do believe when you put a microscope to it. Make a list of false beliefs that keep you energetically "stuck." Addictions are a dead giveaway you have a set of false beliefs needing a close look. Be aware that some of these beliefs can be unconscious. They justify the continuation of the addiction and the reasons you can't stop or can't seek assistance. Addictions are as much an energetic dysfunction as they are physical compulsion. They signal an energy blockage that causes the misdirecting of energy into some other unproductive discharge.

Once you've made your list of false beliefs, you should next explore the emotions these beliefs create. How do these beliefs make you feel? Wallow in all that negative energy that you have stirred up. Now start to forgive yourself. You've already started the healing by understanding and acknowledging the beliefs controlling you. So write down all the messages of forgiveness that come to mind. Allow compassion and love to flow over you. Thank these beliefs for what they are teaching you. Then let's add some perspective to the picture. How many of these beliefs are actually real and how many are just a creation of your overactive ego/intellect? And what purpose are they serving?

Lastly, begin to create affirmations that reflect the healed you and repeat them daily. For example, I visualize and affirm, "I am developing healthy, moderate eating habits that will maintain my weight at a healthful and attractive level," and "Today, I am choosing to eat only those foods that contribute to my overall health."

Do this exercise for each area of your life: work/money, relationships, health, self-judgment, etc. The journey of self-knowledge is a truly exciting and empowering expedition.

Secondly, quit that silly self-talk! The truth is, we don't need it and we can quit! You can turn off your brain, like you turn off your TV. Think of the decision to do so like flipping a switch. Why worry about the future? You can't influence it by dwelling on all the negative possible outcomes. Actually, you can but not in the way that you want. The past is gone. It doesn't do any good to dredge it up. Second guessing any situation is fruitless. You've already learned the lessons the past had to offer. And no one needs to listen to a voice that keeps pointing out our failures or perceived shortcomings. It just keeps us stuck. The wonderful book *Loving What Is* by Byron Katie chronicles her journey from mental breakdown to spiritual wise woman by simply recognizing she could turn off the negative self-talk in her head, and just embrace the glory of reality. Living in reality instead of living in your head is a wonderful relief. You find life is much more enjoyable because you smell the roses instead of thinking ahead to next year's planting. We have the choice to listen to the voice or simply saying to ourselves: "This is unnecessary for me to dwell upon. I'm turning off the switch. Let's enjoy what is before me or just think positive thoughts."

Third, take responsibility for your own health. This doesn't mean to walk away from all doctors and healers. Many of them can help in this process, though it still requires your participation. But it does mean exploring what emotions and memories are inhibiting your health. Fear is the basis of all ill health. Usually it is fear about not having one of the key basic human needs fulfilled — love, acceptance, security, self-esteem. Your body is giving you a message that you need to heal this part of yourself. If you need help, ask the Universe to give you a message about what this pain or illness is trying to convey. I learned that my stomach problems and food allergies had to do with my fear of releasing control. Once I acknowledged this, and began trusting the Universe more, much of my discomfort dissolved.

In healing your emotional ills you must first find out what ails you from an energetic standpoint. Then you have to embrace the old emotions, fears and memories, acknowledge and thank them. If you have unfinished business, express it in a constructive manner. Maybe even seek out the person who helped create the issue and talk it through with compassion and respectful dialogue. Then release the powerful forces holding you back and contributing to your illness. Say goodbye to your old "pals," hand them a suitcase and send them off with a hug. Fill that void with transforming self-love and acceptance. Trust the Universe to help in your healing. By releasing all of the negative energy, you'll be attracting positive healing energy and speeding up your recovery.

Fourth, it may be a paradox, but you must go inside to get outside. Meditation is the most healing act you can perform for your body and your mind. Maybe you don't need to go to an ashram and sit cross-legged on a yoga mat. This just means quieting your mind, reconnecting with your spirit and with the Universe. Once you minimize the chattering noise in your head, you can open yourself to hear the messages the Universe has to offer, the guidance, the wisdom and creativity available to you. It allows you to hear your true self — the peaceful, joyous, happy, self-confident self. Quiet introspection prepares the soil for planting, creating the positive visions that can gracefully take root, transforming your life and the world.

Fifth, four specific elements contribute mightily to the spiritual, mental and physical well-being of an individual — eating healthful foods, exercising, creating time for fun and being outside in nature.

The body craves good food — the right foods. Eating junk food and sitting at a desk all day, every day are energetic time bombs. Not only do these contribute to ill health, they serve to restrict the flow of positive energy into and through your system. Foods to avoid include sugar, wheat, meat, dairy and sodas. Muscle testing — a system widely in practice today with chiropractors and alterative healthcare providers — asks the body to signal its energetic acceptance or resistance to various stimuli, including foods. Those five substances show an immediate weakening of the body when exposed to anyone's system. Fueling the body with fresh foods and relying more on vegetables, poultry, fish and fruit is the most soul-strengthening path to health.

Exercise is equally important. But this doesn't necessarily mean boot camp workouts. The best way to exercise is to do something that you enjoy and thus will motivate you to do more of it. Walking, dancing, swimming, hiking, yoga, basketball, tennis, bicycling — whatever gives you joy — at least three times a week. One of my favorite exercises is to run in the deep part of the pool to pulsating music, wearing a lifejacket. I never touch bottom. It's fun and since I'm not running on pavement, it doesn't jar my bones.

Play is often overlooked as an essential element for balance in our lives. Pressed to do all the things we have "scheduled" into our days, many of us haven't left time for ourselves. Play can be inline skating at the beach, playing cards with friends, taking a walk with your children, going to a movie, reading a book, participating in a favorite hobby, buying a new item for a favorite collection. The soul seeks joy, fun and passion to reconnect with the essential source energy and nourish the original childlike part of us. It's like recharging a battery.

Most of all, we humans need the solace and joy of nature. If you ask 90% of people when they feel most "alive" you'll find they will tell you it is when they are outdoors. The sun is an important source of positive energy as is the earth, the moon, the greenery, the flowers, the rocks and the living creatures. When outside we are among friends. We must take the time to appreciate the grandeur of the Universe. Being awestruck by the beauty of nature — by a glorious multicolored sunset — tends to keep people in the moment, in the presence of reality, instead of in their heads living somewhere in the future or the past. While outdoors, all the space around us and inside us radiates with positive energy in a constantly flowing and recharging interaction. Meditating outdoors in nature is like getting supercharged with spirit.

The most significant contribution anyone can make to the global good is to be happy, joyful, passionate, loving and vitally alive. By clearing out the blockages — mental, spiritual and physical — you are becoming the person the Universe intended you to be.

Global Implications

Clearing the impediments to happiness is the most self-transforming and heroic deed a person can perform. Because in cleaning up the debris on the inside, we are paving the path to peace on the outside. By acting from joy, passion and self-love, we are in the most powerful position to channel the Universe's supreme healing energy outward through our visions, thoughts and actions. We now take our place among the creators — acknowledging that we have an active role in the transformation of the planet. We inject our happiness into the cosmos and magnify it with others to create that place of wonder and peace that is awaiting our call.

UNIVERSAL GUIDING PRINCIPLE 12:
Ask and You Shall Receive; So What Is It I Really Want?

Universal energy is INTELLIGENT ENERGY, it's most extraordinary and exciting aspect. It has the ability to carry with it information. "Connected" individuals, those who can tap into this source — such as psychics, mediums and channelers — can access the Universe's storehouse of information at will. But so can the average "conscious" person, who seeks guidance and wisdom.

No doubt you have at some point experienced a "gut feeling" that turned out to be right, or you sensed "intuition" pointing you in a specific direction. Remember those eerie moments of déjà vu? These are all experiences that result from tapping into the Universal Intelligence for a fleeting moment. Why not then hone the skill that enables us to gain such knowledge whenever and wherever we want it? That would be like having a sage on our shoulder, helping us make smart, wise and energetically responsible decisions.

Learning to tune into your intuition is simple and easy, but it takes "conscious" thought and focused awareness. The first step is to find a place where there is total quiet at a time when you won't have interruptions. Lie down or sit, and breathe deeply. Clear your mind. Shoo out all the busy thoughts and put a clamp on the chatter. Just let your mind's eye stare into the blackness. Then ask a question to which you'd like to have an answer. (Keep in mind this doesn't necessarily work for personal gain, such as picking the winning horse at Santa Anita!)

Select a question that will help you make a choice. "Do I make my presentation to the boss now — or wait a month?" "Is it in my highest good to have this surgery?" "What is the best time to call my mother?" Stay quiet and then wait for an answer. Sometimes it will come then. Other times, you may experience it over the next several days in signs, songs or words from people in idle conversation. Consider those amazing coincidences that just seem to happen — you need an expert in pet behavior? Suddenly, you meet one at a social function.

You are sending out a request and it will come back. You must look for it vigilantly. You must actively participate in the process. It is part of taking responsibility. Sometimes the answer may seem "disguised" in other experiences or messages. Many people hear or see the answers as images in their heads, thinking it is their own thoughts.

It took me a month or two to distinguish between knowledge I had and knowledge that was being "downloaded" to me in answer to my questions. I learned these "downloaded" answers are unfailingly correct and frequently outside the realm of my knowledge base. Now that I've become accustomed to seeking answers, I use it also for solving minor day-to-day problems. "Now where did I put that key ring?" "Under what category did my colleague file that document?" I have been astonished to find the answers readily at hand when I concentrate on sending and receiving them. If you want to improve on this skill, there are a number of excellent books on developing one's intuition, but one of the best is *Practical Intuition* by Laura Day.

Many individuals report that when working on a creative project they have moments of great inspiration when they feel as if the images, words, etc. are just coming through them. It's as if they are "channeling" a higher power. That experience is the result of a direct "information download" from the Universe, where the receiver has opened the door to allow creativity to come forth. Creative inspiration is the combined intelligence of the Universe filtered through the receiver, shaping it to his or her own vision. The Universe is a 24/7 databank…always open for those in quest of an answer that will help them have a healthier, happier, more positive life lived in the light. That's why asking your body why you experience pain or illness in a certain locality will yield answers. That's also why asking for guidance will help one make better, wiser, more life-supporting decisions. But once you ask for guidance, it's better not to ignore it. Should you disregard it, you are likely to experience roadblocks and obstacles on your chosen path. Some people ask for guidance and if it doesn't comply with what they wanted to hear, they discredit it. The guidance is a truth you may not want to hear, but is sent to you for your highest good.

I personally asked the question "What is my higher purpose?" The answer I received is that it is my "destiny" or "mission" to write this book and to begin United World Healing, a non-profit organization designed to bring the globe's people together to create a better world through visualization and action. If you are floundering, not happy in your work, experiencing a mid-life crisis — ask the question "What is your life's purpose?" You might be amazed at the answer!

In order to manifest the desires we want to have in our lives, we must be clear on what we want. Many times we may THINK we want something, when in fact a little voice in the back of our head is sabotaging that dream. Or we may simply be confused by the choices. Asking the Universe for answers helps to obtain clarity. Never hesitate to ask: "What do I really want?" or "What is in my highest good?" Better clear up the confusion and clearly manifest your desire, than complain the Universe is not listening when it doesn't arrive. The Universe can't fulfill your dreams when it's getting dual messages. ("I want this, but I'm not willing to give up that" or "I want this, but I really don't believe I'm worthy of it.")

The key steps in manifesting are knowing with clarity what it is that you wish to bring forth and setting an intention. Visualize it. Take steps to move in that direction, trusting the Universe to bring it forth. Expect it to arrive and be grateful. Therefore, you can see that knowing what you want to achieve is the first essential step in the process. If you need it, there's a Universal expert waiting to you help you!

Global Implications

The more in touch we are with ourselves and the Universe, the easier it is to live a life of joy, peace and prosperity. Following guidance helps us make wise choices, which include choices about the global good. Says Shakti Gawain in her book *The Path of Transformation*: "If you are trusting your intuition and following your heart — going where your energy takes you and doing what you really want to do — you will see that *everything you do has a positive effect in changing the world.*"[8]

UNIVERSAL GUIDING PRINCIPLE 13:
The Balance of Masculine and Feminine

Each of us has within a combination of "masculine and feminine" energies. In a sense, we humans are androgynous creatures, but most of us tilt more strongly toward one direction or another. That may be as a result of association with our sex, but not always. Many homosexual or transgender people have strong energies more closely associated with the opposite sex. In another example of embracing the opposite energy, "tomboy" girls show the influence of masculine energy surfacing at an early age. Ultra-masculine men have suppressed their female energies. Ultra-feminine women have refused to give any quarter to their masculine energy.

Science equates the masculine with left brain analytical thinking and the feminine with the right brain creative and artistic influence. Neither can operate alone. It is in the integration of the two that we have a healthy, functioning human being. But the balance of these two "yin and yang" energies is evident in more than just humans. According to Dr. Norman Milanovich and Dr. Shirley McCune in *The Light Shall Set You Free*: "Masculine and feminine energies are found on all planes — physical, mental and spiritual. Gender refers to a division of labor or effort, which is required for all creativity. Gender is found in organic, as well as inorganic matter and within the operations of heat, light, electricity, magnetism, attraction, repulsion, etc. In each instance, both masculine and feminine energies are essential — the masculine energy directs itself to the feminine energy, thereby initiating the creative process. The feminine energy is the one doing the active creative work." [9]

A spiritually and emotionally healthy human being embraces both energies, creating balance and blending the creative feminine with the intellectual male energy. They are each necessary for the realization of a consciously creative life. Favoring one energy extremely over the other means that one aspect is being suppressed or denied. The result is unhappiness at best, dysfunction at worst and stifles the creative process. By hating or denying one half of ourselves, we are unconsciously sending negative energies into the Universe. Embracing both feminine and masculine energies — accepting, honoring and blending them — propels one toward Conscious Creation.

Global Implications

In an outstanding book, *You Just Don't Understand,* by Dr. Deborah Tannen, a professor of linguistics at Georgetown University, her research discloses how differently men and women see the world. She discovered through their choice of words and their tone that men view the world as a hierarchy — always seeking to position themselves above the next man or woman on the rung. Women on the other hand see themselves as facilitators, bringing others to them in an effort to inspire cooperation or to reach out for assistance. They are collaborative.

Hence, it is easy to see the results of male domination in the world today. The impact of male energies run amok, untempered by the conciliatory wisdom and cooperative nature of women leaders or men who honor their female side, has created a place where might has the upper hand and is valued accordingly.

There are, however, very significant signs that this status quo is changing. The feminist movement of the '70s and '80s forced a reevaluation of gender roles across the globe. Today we have a growing generation of men far more comfortable with their feminine energies and women who are equally embracing both elements as they navigate the working world and home life. On a global basis countries are increasingly electing female leadership at all levels of government. Recently, a woman became Speaker of the House of Representatives, the third most powerful position in the government behind The President and Vice President. A growing number of nations have women prime ministers, presidents or political leaders including France, Chile and Germany.

If we are to envision and realize a peaceful and economically healthy world, it will mean drawing far more from the feminine energy of cooperation and love. We will need to honor men and women equally and envision ways to free the millions of women oppressed by religious and other regimes. That world will need to unite men and women in cooperative ventures for the betterment of every community and mankind at large.

UNIVERSAL GUIDING PRINCIPLE 14:
'Tis Greater to Give Than Receive, but Receiving Is Pretty Nice, Too!

If we were not consumed with the daily responsibilities of making a living and supporting ourselves or our families — if completely provided for — the majority of people on this planet would choose to spend their spare time and money helping someone else. Look at the billions of dollars raised for charities, causes and crisis relief. Today's growth of the non-profit sector in terms of both donations and volunteerism is unprecedented. With each disaster comes an outpouring of love, money and support for the victims, whether they are in Indonesia or New Orleans. Or just down the street.

Unhindered by the challenges of daily life or the competitiveness of "getting ahead," fully realized human beings have a basic desire to help — to be "of service." This is the essence of Universal love that is present in all of us, our basic nature before we load everything else in from the material world on top of it. There is a good Samaritan in each of us.

The sharing of one's time, wealth, home, advice or labor with an individual less privileged is mankind's ongoing, greatest act of love. And it is fully supported by the Universe. For each person who makes a commitment to give, he, too, will receive in equal or more measure.

Don't be surprised, however, if the return comes in a slightly different form. Money given may result in a return of advice that stimulates more money. Or time given may result in less labor at work, so the giver can have more leisure time at home.

The recipients of your largess can be family, friends, lovers, neighbors or strangers. One act of kindness resonates with the world. You don't need to formally volunteer at the local hospital, just take your grandmother out for ice cream once a week. Giving is a blessing in any form to anyone and begins to change the world one act at a time.

Global Implications

In the world we want to experience, no one is alone and everyone has a support system. Today, though, the streets are filled with homeless, children are dying from starvation in Third World countries, adults can't read in 10% of the world, people are dying from diseases because no one cares or has money to cure them. There is clearly so much need. While we are visualizing, we can also act. The joy in the gift, blesses the giver and the receiver. We can each give rein to the natural part of us that wants to help by applying our resources as a concerted conscious effort to assist others. The positive energy that we emit in so doing attracts abundance for us and for the world at large.

UNIVERSAL GUIDING PRINCIPLE 15:
Claiming Your "Stuff"

Your life is what you have made it — consciously or unconsciously. In order to reach our own point of empowerment, each one of us must acknowledge that we are the creators of the reality we experience. Whether that is a life predominantly lived in joy and contentment or one dominated by pain and struggle. The good news is we can change it as soon as we begin Consciously Creating, molding it to be the life we choose.

Clearing the way to Conscious Creation, however, means releasing any feelings of being a victim or blaming others for how our lives have turned out. We have to "claim our stuff." If you have been victimized, somehow energetically you have attracted that treatment to yourself, put yourself in a place that it can happen, lacked the confidence to speak up for yourself, entrusted someone else instead of trusting your better judgment, etc. No one can take advantage of you unless you have given him or her the power to do so. We are far from powerless creatures and must remember that daily.

Claiming "your stuff," though, also means you shouldn't claim anyone else's "stuff." People can be mean, petty, petulant, deliberately hurtful and selfish. They can exhibit all kinds of negative energies. They may even be your relatives! You have a choice: you can get down on their level and engage or you can choose to stay in your positive energy mind frame. You can buy into their name calling directed toward you, their opinions about all the ways they think you have failed — or not. The minute you participate on their level, you lower your own energy level. The best defense is NONE. Ignore them. Let them have their opinions. If there's validity, then "own your stuff." If there's no validity, than throw a net of love out and see what happens, change the topic, ignore them or try to avoid such people in the future. You don't have to argue, respond or internalize. You know the truth and that's all that matters. Let it guide you.

This is also a helpful lesson in remembering that you cannot live someone else's life. If someone is intent on self-destruction or wallowing in personal misery you can offer help, but no one can truly rescue someone else. Don't get swept up taking on someone else's "stuff," because you feel sorry for them or love them so much you want to fix it. This is their stuff, NOT YOURS.

As powerful creators we acknowledge that once we are the source of our own reality, we can let go of the need to be a victim or to blame others. Let other people have their realities. We need to reserve our energies for manifesting a better future for The Universe and ourselves.

Global Implications

If only we now can prevent politicians and governments from pointing fingers, we might get somewhere! The blame game is a giant energetic roadblock. A perfect example is the war in Iraq. If the U.S. administration had expended the huge dollars on poverty, health or alternative fuels in this country instead of blaming Saddam Hussein for 9/11, think of what we might have accomplished? Many nations would rather blame others than accept responsibility for how the world is today. And certainly they are far more willing to engage in finding fault than they are in solution finding. It's time for them to let go of these old habits. Then we can all jump on the Universal superhighway to world improvement.

UNIVERSAL GUIDING PRINCIPLE 16:
Being All Three — Judge, Jury and Convict

Judgment is a double-edged sword. If you are judging others, you are most assuredly judging yourself. The act of judgment is the antithesis of unconditional love. It poisons relationships and divides people, rather than uniting them. Gossip is a particularly hurtful form of judgment because it is expressed in words, not just held in thought, and it is easily disseminated to spread the damage.

In changing one's life to be a Conscious Creator, one needs to look very carefully at the prejudices one holds and the ways we can disrespect others, discount people and ignore them as being unworthy of our attention. Even the ill-dressed clerk at the local convenience store has gifts of which you may not be aware unless you spend some time talking. Everyone is worthy of regard, compassion and acceptance. Look deeply and you can find the goodness in almost everyone — even for instance a gang banger. Treat someone with regard and they often rise to fulfill those expectations. Treat them with disregard and they will flounder, strike out with resentment or prove to be the disappointment you projected onto them.

Frequently when we judge, we project our least desired traits onto others. If we fear appearing weak, we judge others to be weak. It's a tip-off that we have a judgment against ourselves we are harboring. Time to explore our inner prejudice. The strong emotions that others elicit in us generally mean we are denying a part of ourselves. This part needs to be brought out in the light, examined, honored and accepted before we can release the need to judge.

In looking clearly at ourselves we see that most of us spend enormous amounts of time being self-critical when we should each be celebrating our wonderful assets! A major step on the road to becoming a Conscious Creator is letting go of judgment altogether. No one said that it's an easy task, but the benefits are truly remarkable. You begin with extending love and compassion to yourself, accepting who you are, embracing all of your attributes and features then forgiving any past judgment. Just revel in being you!

Next, undertake extending unconditional love to just about everyone else! Let go of the need to be right because this is something that implies you believe you are superior to others. Respect other people's entitlement to their opinion. When acting in love and acceptance you are tapping into the Universe's natural state. You will find yourself attracting acceptance in return everywhere you go.

Letting go of judgment moves us forward with a giant step. It allows us to create a fresh start, a new beginning without the negative energy of judgment clouding our horizon, filtering out the sunlight. Release judgment against others and yourself — and let the light in.

Global Implications

Racism, sexism, religious intolerance and ethnic strife — these are all mankind's judgments played out on a global scale. It says, "I am better than him or her." Judgment is the most divisive energy on the planet, a most potent manifestation of fear.

If I am equal to my brother, we share certain values and experiences, and I must respect his humanity. We can work together. If I am superior to my brother then I can dominate him and belittle his humanity. If I am inferior to my brother, I have to look up to him and bow to his will.

The act of elevating one's self or feeling inferior polarizes people, stimulating conflict. By holding others as "different" — better or worse — we stop the positive energy flow between us. This disconnect allows negative energy to fill the void, damaging ourselves, the relationship between peoples and the Earth.

UNIVERSAL GUIDING PRINCIPLE 17:
Making Friends With The Present

Remember those moments when you feel most "alive?" Those are special times when you are experiencing the present moment and tuning into the Universal force. Such moments carry piercingly powerful positive emotions. You are not worrying about the future, nor rehashing the past. You are right there, just enjoying that moment, conscious of only the stimulus to your senses and the exciting emotion that stimulus creates.

Wouldn't life be better if we could just live every day in this state of euphoria? We can, actually. By simply choosing to live in the "now."

All that useless mind chatter we hear in our heads is wrapped up in the future and the past.

- ° *How can I get back at my co-worker for sabotaging me? (future)*
- ° *My last lover cheated on me and I just can't stop thinking about it. (past)*
- ° *I'm worried about my mother's illness. (future)*
- ° *I feel guilty for not spending more time with my family. (past)*
- ° *Will I have enough money for the house payment? (future)*
- ° *Can I lose weight for my birthday party? (future)*
- ° *I hate the fact I haven't lost twenty-five pounds. (past)*

All that matters is right now. Live it. Love it. Experience it. Yes, you must act now to impact your future, but *worrying* about the future and living in the past take up huge amounts of energy that can be put toward Conscious Creation and enjoying the satisfaction of the moment. Accepting what is and then embracing it is exhilarating…it's freeing! Let go of the past and the future and you can experience the now. Two excellent and groundbreaking books on this topic are Eckhart Tolle's *The Power of Now* and Byron Katie's *Loving What Is.*

So how can you do this?

- ° When those past/future thoughts come into your mind, don't fixate or obsess. Lovingly release them. Acknowledge them for past help, and then say, "I let you go." Then gently shut the door and turn your attention to right now!

- ° Rather than fixate on the future or worry about it, change it. Use Conscious Creation to visualize what you'd like to happen then let it go and forget about it. Get back to the present.

° Take more time to appreciate the present moment as if you were a person observing yourself. *I am enjoying writing this e-mail to my best friend. I love singing in the shower. I am so excited by the new blooms on my rose bush. I am really happy with this report I have written for my client. I love this meeting with my co-workers — we are operating on all cylinders. This restaurant is fantastic. What an incredible sunset! I love seeing my daughter laugh. This is a precious moment with my husband. I have learned a lesson in this experience and I will apply what I've learned in the future. What a blessing!*

The special gift of living in the now — and experiencing the joy in doing so — is the new positive energy you are magnetizing to yourself. Living in the now is the gift that keeps on giving. By experiencing *this very moment,* you are keeping that portal to the Universe open.

Global Implications

The world and our leadership are so mired in the past and past habits they have forsaken today. In this very moment we must let go of the past that binds us and restricts our thinking, embrace today and then create for tomorrow.

Without holding onto past wrongs, impediments, limitations — and dwelling in these, we can re-envision new paths to the future. In this moment free of negative thinking, we can *make change* for the future, *visualize change* for the future and *create* the future. Our point of power is now.

UNIVERSAL GUIDING PRINCIPLE 18:
Actions Speak Louder Than ~~Words~~...Just Visualizing

Vision *and* action unified are the most powerful combination for manifesting. They are synergistic, amplifying the energy and power of the creator. The Universe first experiences the benefit of your positive thinking that leads to the act and then the positive energy created by the act. This is an energetic double whammy!

When you act in the material world, this shows the universe that you are willing to "walk the talk," that you are ready to carry out your intent and participate in the act of creation. While visualization is a very powerful tool for creating your future, taking action speeds that future in coming to you. For example, visualizing a harmonic relationship with a fractious relative is a very valuable way to engage the Universe's assistance in creating that harmony. Extending an olive branch, however, by inviting that relative to lunch on your dime for a heart-to-heart chat may in fact make that healing come to fruition a lot faster. Again, the old adage "God helps those who help themselves" applies to this principle.

Action is also change. By taking action we signal the Universe that we are ready to accept change and to create it at the same time. We are planting the seeds for our own transformation when we act to transform what is outside of us. Setting an intention and following through with love, kindness and compassion creates the most fertile environment for growing the life we want to enjoy.

Global Implications

It is exciting to see the many nonprofit organizations around the world that have made vision combined with action a cornerstone of their mission in their respective area of emphasis. Whether that be for eradicating disease, human rights, environmental sustenance, wildlife protection and recovery, eliminating hunger, etc., people are coming together to create a better world. The only *caveat* is the negative energy that emerges if an organization tips the balance into violence or divisive rhetoric instead of peaceful, yet powerful strategies. This will hinder the well-intended mission.

This guiding principle is also true for governments. Acting out of a conscious higher vision will always bring a speedier and more desirable result than violence or arm-twisting. Resistance is strewn across the path if the intent is negative. The Universe supports action that has a basis in global good.

UNIVERSAL GUIDING PRINCIPLE 19:
Constant Education — Oh, Those Tests!

What do you do when bad things happen to you? Curse at others, beat yourself up for your own stupidity, go into a deep depression or feel the world is ganging up on you? We should recognize these are all wrong responses. The right one is to ask: "What lesson is the Universe trying to teach me?"

Everything, indeed, does happen for a reason. Our lives are our schoolrooms. They offer tests by the Universe to see how we negotiate energetic roadblocks and how we use our power — or fail to do so. According to Dr. Norman Milanovich and Dr. Shirley McCune in *The Light Shall Set You Free*: "The Higher Self is programmed to fill each void (frequency) that has not been learned or mastered with experiences needed to assure personal growth."[7] As we climb toward higher consciousness and energetic harmony with the Universe, we are presented with opportunities to demonstrate our awareness and knowledge. If we fail the test, we are destined to repeat it again, maybe in different ways and under different circumstances, but just as painfully as the previous time. We cannot go on to a higher frequency if we haven't mastered the previous level, any more than we can get to the top rung of the ladder by bypassing the lower ones leading to it. We have to work through the Karma involved or transform our negative energy patterns into positive ones before we can advance.

Challenges are opportunities to test our newfound wisdom. A crisis frequently precedes transformation; it has the ability to compel us to examine our beliefs and to act in new ways. We even sometimes unconsciously create our own crisis in order to draw in change, to force ourselves to come face-to-face with what we must do to transform. Change nudges us to move into a higher realm, helping us to evolve. It's an opportunity to see whether we can raise our frequency or whether we are not yet ready to make the leap. That itself should be incentive to do what is necessary to be ready for that leap.

When we encounter problems, challenges or obstacles, the questions to ask are:

- ° As the powerful creator that I am, why have I manifested this experience?

- ° What must I do in order to move forward and transform this into a positive learning experience?

- ° What is the valuable lesson to be learned?

Once you begin reframing your experiences in this light, you will find faster and easier solutions to challenges. By viewing challenges as learning experiences sent to assist you, you will open the pathway to Universal knowledge that helps you obtain the answers you seek. Furthermore, you will also discover that fewer "unwelcome" challenges find their way to your doorstep.

You must also begin seeing relationships in much the same way. Every person who comes into your life is here to help you learn and grow. That could be someone who teaches you to be more loving, or it could be a lover who treats you poorly. Each of these people has a lesson to teach you about yourself. What you take away from the experience will determine whether you are on a path toward high-frequency growth or merely stuck.

Global Implications

One could view so many horrible and heinous acts of mankind as failed trials showing our species has yet to learn to live by the golden rule. And indeed that may be the case. But such a track record can also set the stage for a quantum leap in learning if we choose.

Each time our world faces a crisis we are given the opportunity to make choices that will heal or tear apart our planet. Such a "test" presents a turning point when we call forth the action and vision leading to a path of peace and mutual respect. It's a renewed opportunity for humankind to prove itself — to stand for healing and a better world. As humanity becomes more conscious and people of all races, nationalities and economic status begin to recognize their innate power, we have the ability to be the "teachers" helping the rest of the globe to recognize and pass the tests presented to us. It is incumbent on us to stand up and speak, to help create this shift by awakening others.

UNIVERSAL GUIDING PRINCIPLE 20:
Perfection Exists — It's Buried Here Somewhere

Imagine an alternative universe where everything is perfect. You have a perfectly healthy and weight-appropriate body; the world is at peace. Lovely neighbors surround you. Your bank account has ample money for retirement, etc. Now here's the thing: that perfect universe exists. It just exists in the world we cannot yet see in the Universe of infinite possibilities. Conscious Creation can align all of the key elements in one place, defining reality out of a probability. Through transformation we lift the veil on the invisible world and call it forth into reality.

Remember that perfect house you envisioned and then one day, there it was — available for you to purchase? How about the perfect pet that you had in mind? Next thing you knew there was a kitty on your doorstep. Coincidence isn't coincidence. It's opening the veil between you and the perfect universe, bringing forth your heartfelt desire into reality. You've done it through the power of vision and cleansing, high-frequency energy. Just think of the amazing life to be lived in Universal perfection. It's not that far removed from us!

Global Implications

The world of peace and abundance for all is simply waiting until enough human souls call it forth. As humanity begins to clear away the muck of our unenlightened consciousness, the shining world will become visible.

UNIVERSAL GUIDING PRINCIPLE 21:
Learning to Trust and Surrender

Want to know the fastest way to manifest miracles in your life? Turn it over to the Universe. Trusting the Universe to bring whatever is in your highest good will in fact deliver what you need or desire most. Note that I say "need" because what you receive may also be a useful lesson that helps you reach the next level of frequency. It could also be a rescue from a dangerous situation or recovery from a serious illness. The Universe seeks to protect us and lead our spirits to the light. The key is that we must surrender to its knowledge of our best interests. By seeking to "control" our fates, we block the Universe's goodwill and protection. Control is an emotion that arises from fear, demonstrating a complete lack of faith in the Universe. We fear that we must maintain the control — or our lives will spin away and we will be at the mercy of an unforgiving unknown future. That's a very negative vision of the future. On the contrary, trust in the Universe is an optimistic vision and positive energy that attracts similar positive frequencies.

Trust in the Universe lets us venture into new exciting uncharted territories, leaving our place of safety, knowing that whatever comes will be right for us. It allows for change to come into our lives that may at first seem strange or stressful but will ultimately prove to be for our benefit. So, meeting change without resistance, accepting it and surrendering to it as a gift from the Universe will bring a quick adjustment and greater serenity.

Trust is a critical step in the process of manifesting. When we want to manifest what we desire we must envision it, experience the joy of having it arrive in our lives then let it go and trust the Universe will bring it to us. Obsessing over it, trying to force it, worrying about it, will never work. These are all negative controlling energies that clog the delivery channel. Just trust and surrender. Then watch things fall into place with coincidences, synchronicities and surprises. Your wish will come trickling, speeding or serendipitously into your life.

Global Implications

As we go about manifesting a better world, there will be setbacks. We must trust these are for a reason and the Universe will guide us toward the light. We must not get discouraged by seeming impediments and instead take solace in the knowledge that there is value in the journey itself.

UNIVERSAL GUIDING PRINCIPLE 22:
Gratitude — The Universal "Juice"

Gratitude is like the WD40® of the Universe...it makes everything run smoother. One of the highest frequencies on the scale, gratitude, confirms to the Universe that you are worthy of its largess. Thankfulness is rewarded in turn with more things for which to be thankful. The purpose of being thankful, however, should not be to gain more, but to simply be appreciative for the blessings we are given.

Here are a few items that people often take for granted and which beg to be remembered with gratitude:

- Your home

- Your work

- Your loved ones

- Your health

- Your relationship with the Universe

- Your freedom

- Nature and beauty

- The GOOD that is occurring in the world

- Your existence

The last one is particularly important. Be thankful for each breath you take because this life is a gift. We often overlook the simple blessing of living, and it's important that we express gratitude for the ability to think, feel and be. Our existence as human beings is an immense gift from the Universe.

Remembering to be grateful as we live our busy lives is oftentimes neglected. Most people do this at church, when saying grace at dinner on Thanksgiving Day before cutting the turkey or in great moments of celebration such as weddings and births. We can do better. Three practices come to mind that might make gratitude more ingrained in one's existence.

- Give yourself a Gratitude Moment every day at the same time. Ask yourself "what do I have to be grateful for?" and then thank the Universe.

- Have a Gratitude List and add to it regularly with every new benefit, fortune, friend, experience that comes your way.

° Go outside on a beautiful sunny day, raise your face to the sky and recite thanks for all the things that give you joy and make your life worth living.

Gratitude is not just between you and the Universe. It should be expressed toward others as well. Little words of recognition and thanks are a way of honoring others for what they contribute to your life. Take a moment to thank someone for a task he or she does automatically for you without expecting a return — like the postman for example — and watch the smile arrive!

Global Implications

A major dose of gratitude by all of the world's peoples is long overdue. Too often we believe that we "have earned what we have on our own" and we "deserve it." Especially among young people today, one finds a sense of entitlement by those who have been spoiled by the affluent world in which they grew up. We often take for granted those people who provide services for us — who clean our houses, bag our groceries, cut our lawns. Gratitude is in short supply. We need to get it flowing on every level and in every society.

UNIVERSAL GUIDING PRINCIPLE 23:
The Power of the Person

Each one of us has an infinite power to impact others on this planet. While it is easy to throw our hands up and say, "I'm just one person," history has shown us the power of a single individual with the vision, energy and self-awareness to change the world. Self-empowerment *is* global empowerment.

As we awaken to our power of consciousness creation, we ignite, change and touch others. By tossing out our net of love and kindness, we transform situations from negative to positive. Our frequencies reach out and merge, mingle and transmute other energies that set off new chain reactions.

By creating and following our own vision, others follow. The power of our spiritual vision is only second to the Universe. We are the ultimate creators. Through our intent, we become the vehicle of the Universe to manifest its light on Earth, and we create that better world. Conscious Creation is catching. You can spread it through thoughts, words, deeds and leadership.

Over the years and through the complexities of daily life, we lost the awareness of our own power. As we are rousing ourselves from the sleep of unconsciousness — from victimhood, powerlessness or self-destruction — the new knowledge of our power and impact is stunning and awe-inspiring.

It is imperative that we learn to use it in the right way, not exclusively for our personal gain but for the mutual benefit of the planet's other inhabitants and the Earth as a whole. With this power comes responsibility to teach, empower others, speak up and envision.

Knowing your own power and how to wield it in concert with the Universe is a great gift and makes you one of the magnificent creators. It gives you freedom and a joyful responsibility.

Global Implications

Goethe once said, "Dream no small dreams, for they have no power to move the hearts of men." Each of us can be an engine for betterment in the grand machine. We have the power to improve our own lives, which will by itself have resonance on a global level. We can each take it one step further if we couple our Conscious Creation with action in the material world, by volunteering, becoming an agent of change or by imbuing love where there was none before. And most significantly, we can join with others to raise our vision and our voice in the new consciously awakening world, raising the amplitude and magnifying the power of energy for change.

UNIVERSAL GUIDING PRINCIPLE 24:
Why Are We Here?

The simple answer is that we are here to evolve. The ultimate goal is to raise our frequency high enough through our acts, our right choices, our positive thoughts and emotions to meld with the Universal power of love, harmony, peace and serenity. We are the bridge between the world we see and the world beyond. While achieving higher consciousness will ultimately bring joy and happiness to our personal lives here on Earth, as we evolve we also become messengers and bringers of the light to the manifest world. Our energy opens the door for more love, peace and harmony to ripple out to everyone we know and the planet at large.

The evolutionary journey, though, is not an easy one. While our core spirits are beings of love, light and wisdom, it may take us a while to recognize this and get back to reality because we are presently in physical form. But our physical existence as human beings offers a unique and powerful opportunity for higher evolution. For most of us, our lives are pretty messy and don't come anywhere near the ideal of such grace. We spend our early years completely self-focused on the excess of youthful acquisitiveness; we spend our thirties and early forties trying to survive financially and support families, and then we finally begin to search for our connection with our spirit and the Universe as we approach our fifties. It's a long journey before we make that reconnect, one where we miss the nourishment of spirit because we are focused elsewhere.

There is no need to wait until our lives are half over to be in touch with who we really are. The Universe sent us here to be agents of its design, to live in joy and bless the Earth with our positive energies and knowledge...and we can do that at any age, at any stage of our Earthly lives. The Universe's intent is for us to be the transforming force in bringing peace, joy and love to all of our cohabitants and to this planet we call Earth.

Global Implications

Almost unanimously in the metaphysical world and mind/body/spirit movement, there is a belief that this period in the first dozen years of the millennium is a transformative period. Humans are awakening to their true role, to their creative power and to the potential of mankind for manifesting a better, peaceful, abundant world. Many people feel this call to action and they experience it happening at an astonishing rate. It is as if the Universe has flipped a switch, calling us out of sleep — deepening people's relationship with their spiritual nature. Do you feel it? We have been given a task to fulfill. Are you ready to take your part in it?

UNIVERSAL GUIDING PRINCIPLE 25:
Humanity is Underrated

Human potential is limitless…The only thing limiting us is belief in our own limits. As you will see in the next chapter, science is uncovering new frontiers of the mind, and this is only the beginning of far greater possibilities. Once we take the blinders off, we will find extraordinary powers. They may involve multi-dimensional interactions, the ability to transport our consciousness and leave our bodies behind, telepathic communications and much more. We have a vast window on the mysteries of the Universe. We have only opened a tiny crack.

Global Implications

As our consciousness evolves and expands, we will have the opportunity to engage in the most remarkable achievements. They have the power to bring us closer to the source energy, to allow us to manifest solutions for our salvation on Earth and lastly to direct our Conscious Creativity to the peaceful interaction between our world and any others we may encounter.

MAKING SCIENCE *of it* ALL

M*ay the Force Be With You.* Actually, it already is! Science is beginning to lift the veil on a sea of energy that not only surrounds us, but is within us as well. This dynamic point of interaction between energy fields is precisely the point where we can imprint our future.

Think of the Universe as a giant pool of energy, where everything seen and unseen is also made of energy. The part that we don't see resonates at a far higher frequency than does visible matter. Science, viewed through the filter of quantum physics, calls this underlying source of energy the Zero Point Field or Unified Field. For our purposes we might think of it as The Universe. Science says it is comprised of the most fundamental basic force or energy from which our world springs. This theory goes one step forward and says that since everything is derived from this unending source of energy, then everything is connected like a cosmic web. When there is a disturbance in one area, the ripple effect is felt all the way out to the far reaches.

Quantum physics — the New Physics — is becoming the key to unlocking the door to the mysteries of the Universe. Where once scientists were confronted by many properties that made no sense if viewed against the historic perspective of Newtonian science, they are now starting to grasp the workings of the subatomic world. In the past few years they have learned that protons can also be waves at the same time and that a subatomic particle can be at two places simultaneously. More importantly, they discovered that particles are really only probabilities until they coalesce as real. According to Dr. Marya Mann in an essay by Geralyn Gendreau in the book *Healing the Heart of the World*, "At a subatomic level, matter does not exist with certainty at definite places but rather shows tendencies to exist. Called probability waves, these potentialities move at light-speed, and when enough of them intersect a new particle is formed. This is known as the Quantum Wave Function or quaff. As agents of free will, we select how and in what direction we want to move and act...focus with conscious intention on particular probability waves gives chosen potentials a set of barbells, builds their strength and constellates particles to bring forth an actuality."[1]

Dr. David Bohm, a pioneering thinker in quantum physics and consciousness, also held this view of the world. He perceived that everything in the Universe is part of an "implicate" order (unseen and in a state of potential to be called forth) until it becomes "explicate" — the reality we know. Thus, the "enfolded or implicate order" is where everything — matter, ideas, thought — originates and gives rise to the "unfolded or explicate order," the world we perceive. Our eyes and our minds only see the unfolded order. But the larger implicate world, though not part of our conscious reality, would be the energetic dimension where all things originate, are stored and exist before they become real to us. Bohm maintains that this larger "wholeness" connects every part and particle of the Universe — from you to the rose in your yard, to the planets and stars, to the space in between. The implication is that we are truly all one — not separate entities living alone on this planet.

In his book *Wholeness and the Implicate Order*, Bohm further viewed the Universe as a hologram where if one portion is broken away, it still holds the image of the whole. In a hologram a laser beam is split. One half is directed to an object where it "captures" an image and then is directed to a holographic plate. On the plate this image is defused and merely looks like a bunch of concentric rings until its other half arrives. When the second half of the beam, bounced off mirrors, strikes the plate, a three-dimensional image of the object suddenly appears. However, if you shatter the holographic plate, even the tiniest portion will contain the complete image of the original object. The interpretation is that in each of us is the blueprint of the original.

Indeed, quantum physics calculations by laser physicist Hal Puthoff begin to bear out the theory of interconnectedness through the Zero Point Field. Within this field, scientists hypothesize, is all of the world's knowledge — past, present and future — because waves are encoders and decoders of information. Thoughts then are structured vibrations that reside in both our "real" world and the Universe at large, an imprint on the Universal energy fabric. Be careful what you think because it may have an infinite life!

While developing the technology for today's Magnetic Resonance Imaging Machine (MRI), Dr. Walter Schempp, a noted math professor at the University of Siegen in Germany may have opened a window on this prospect of the Universe's nature as a vast memory bank. Using what he called "quantum holography" to capture and recreate a 3-D picture of the inside of a human body, Schempp essentially figured out a way to pull information out of the Zero Point Field where it was stored.

One of the most interesting properties of this unlimited energetic cosmos is its striving to reach coherence. Dr. Hubert Frolich, a physicist at the University of Liverpool, showed that once energy reaches a certain level, molecules begin to vibrate until they cohere. That, interestingly enough, is where they begin to act in accordance with the properties of quantum mechanics, including non-locality, a state where one particle is impacted and others not-related to it elsewhere demonstrate the same characteristics.

Every molecule has its own individual frequency, and as it resonates, it attracts its like — it coheres. This motion toward coherence has significance for us because most of us arrive on this planet with coherent personal energy systems. The disruption of that system, the blockage of energy flow, is proving to be what causes illness — first in our energy bodies and then in our physical bodies. As beings of light, our health is indicated by the vitality of molecules, the speed at which we vibrate. Studies show that dying plants, animals and humans show diminishing energy. Higher vibration equals greater health…and as it is becoming equally evident, greater ability to interact with the "enfolded" order, the world as one.

In her extraordinary book, *Infinite Mind, Science of Human Vibrations and Consciousness,* Dr. Valerie Hunt, professor of psychology and physiology at UCLA, noted that her studies revealed the highest frequency energies emitting from individuals who had supreme moments of high consciousness in meditation. Those were the individuals who experienced a great "knowing" of wisdom, a sense of oneness with the Universe, an infinite sense of love and peace. High frequencies would then potentially be the doorway to the Zero Point Field, or "the Universe."

Thus, if we are one with this sea of energy, would it not follow that we are also similarly structured as holistic beings with both "enfolded" and "unfolded" elements? Let's consider our bodies as the "unfolded" reality and our consciousness as the "enfolded" reality. We cannot see consciousness, but this enfolded part of us represents our thoughts, memories, spiritual connection and will. Therefore, how do we begin to perceive the unseen? We look for the energy.

In her years of research in the lab at UCLA, Hunt used very sensitive instruments to measure the energy frequency of a variety of subjects. Among her most significant findings were studies she conducted with healers and those individuals being healed. Simultaneously, while measuring the energetic bio-response of her subjects, she recorded what aura readers were seeing. Fascinatingly, she found the colors the aura readers were describing around the subject's *chakras* correlated exactly to their frequency equivalents — with lower frequencies starting with red, rising to the highest frequency of white light. She also documented the energy emanating from the hands of healers and release of energy from those who had a sudden catharsis, seeing energy flood upward through the crown *chakra*. Here then is the beginning scientific evidence demonstrating that *chakras* and meridians are indeed an integral part of the human energy system and portals of energy entering, absorbing and leaving the body.

After recording distinct differences in the energy emitted by the healer and the ill party before the session, Hunt found at the conclusion that both were emitting the same wavelength. Her research also revealed that a person's energy field — or aura — responded to stimulus *prior* to their minds or bodies, and that bodily dysfunction could be predicted by disturbances in the energy field. Hunt noted a distinction in frequency depending on the range of a person's focus and psychic or spiritual status. Most people were in the lower frequency ranges, but as participants increased in psychic perception, their frequency increased and those who were in the highest states of consciousness through meditation, hypnosis or other natural means, logged in at the top of the chart.

Hunt conducted further studies that placed subjects in a controlled environment and then altered first the electric field and thereafter the magnetic field. An aura reader viewed the experiments and Hunt's instruments recorded the subjects' biofeedback. When reducing either electric or magnetic force, the participants' auric fields became scattered, disorganized and incoherent, and the parties became dysfunctional, disoriented and distressed. When the room was restored to normalcy, each individual's auras coalesced and he or she regained physical balance and sense of well-being. Further, when the field was enhanced above the normal level, the subjects recorded experiencing an expanded consciousness.

Hunt's pioneering research into the personal energy field is profound and revealing. There is a growing school of scientific thought that consciousness and our minds are really in our auric — or as Hunt calls it — Mind-Field, while the brain is merely a recording and retrieval device. Hunt believes that our personal memories are stored in our Mind-Fields and there is a constant transaction going on between the Zero Point Field and the Mind-Field, an ongoing exchange of energy in terms of knowledge, global memory and wisdom. Elsewhere in this book, we incorporate the idea of Hunt's Mind-Field into the overall "Energy Body."

Internal energy communications is also a new frontier in medicine and science today. Dr. Candace Pert, a leading researcher in brain biochemistry at the National Institute of Health, found that some responses between the brain and other parts of our body happen much too fast to be a result of normal cell communication. She attributes this to quantum functions. Neurosurgeon Dr. Karl Pribram has postulated that photons may be shooting across a network of "lightpipes" emanating from the membranes of cells, giving instruction to cells elsewhere in the body at speeds far too high to record. Pribram also proposed that the brain functions as a hologram, just as does the Universe, making us — in effect — smaller, more contained versions of the Universe. If the body is indeed communicating along holistic quantum physics principles implied by Bohm and others, then instantaneous response — "non-locality" — is not out of the realm of possibility in reality as we presently know it.

Biologist Dr. Bruce Lipton reports in his book *The Biology of Belief* that he had a revelation while studying cell membranes and their proteins. Certain proteins have "receptor antennas" that read vibrational energy fields including light, sound and radio frequencies, resonating like tuning forks to stimulus from outside the cell. He maintained that energy vibrating externally could alter the protein's electrical charge, causing it to change shape. Thus, he concluded that cells are programmable and that the programmer lies *outside* the cell. Lipton said, "Biological behavior and gene activity are dynamically linked to information from the environment, which is downloaded into the cell."[2] To Lipton, information from the environment meant the Universe or one's soul. Further, he perceived the brain to be a "central information processor" — in the lingua of computers — and that it could override repetitive habitual cell behavior (i.e. stored memory or beliefs) by providing new input.

The evidence of living energy bodies is not limited to humans. Dr. Harold S. Burr, a neuroanatomist at Yale University, measured electrical fields of plants and animals. Even when a salamander was yet an unfertilized egg, Burr discovered it has an energy field shaped like an adult. He also documented fully adult plant energy fields around tiny seedlings, yet to begin growing. What perfect evidence of Universal intent! Peter Tompkins and Christopher Bird recounted numerous studies of plant energy and the impact of human thought on plants in their book *The Secret Life of Plants*.

Valentina and Seymon Kirlian, Russian researchers known for their technique of photographing the energy emissions of plants and people, found a startling phenomenon in their research. If one cut off a portion of a leaf, the resulting image showed the entire leaf's shape prior to the incision. Dr. Robert O. Becker, an orthopedist looking at electromagnetism in animals, also examined salamanders, finding that there was a surge of energy just before the creature began re-growing a new limb after amputation.

The imprint of energy is in everything. Medicine has long been skeptical at the effectiveness of homeopathy, a form of treatment for medical ailments which employs application of pills or solutions so diluted they contain virtually none of the original compound. Yet Dr. Jacques Benveniste, an M.D. at the University of Paris, conducted seminal studies showing the electromagnetic imprint of the original compound stayed in water diluted hundreds of times — so diluted none of the molecules of the original compound could possibly have been present.

So what other properties of energy and wave behavior impact us as our electrons bounce around the world? For starters the person with the most cohesive wave pattern will influence a person with a lower frequency or less cohesive pattern, bringing them both into a synchronized state, according to researchers. Quieting the analytic left brain through hypnosis or meditation allows the artistic, spiritual, creative right brain to access higher states of consciousness, and – according to a growing number of studies – access more previously unknown information from the Universe. Children under five are naturally more open to receiving such information because they operate in a continual high-frequency state. When two waves get in sync with each other, a process called "constructive wave interference," their signal gets stronger. Thus, when two "thought waves" of intention join together, they multiply their power.

Where does emotion fit into the equation? Hunt maintains that emotions are the "organizers of the energy field." Highly charged emotions direct the flow of energy and, in fact, can lock it into a field. Emotions can cohere molecules; focus brings them together resonating in a powerful lock step. That can mean imprinting memories of high-frequency energies of ecstasy and joy or low-frequency energies of sorrow, self-hate and pain permanently on one's energy body. Negative emotions show up as disturbances in the field, the initial indicator of illness before it manifests in the physical body.

It behooves us to protect this astounding energy synthesizer that we are — to keep it swept clean of negative harmful influences and continue to strive toward evolving to higher frequencies. Some of the more interesting scientific theories posit that injecting fresh new energy into an organic system maintains its energetic health. This prevents the entropy and decay that would come naturally in nature as coherence declines, prompting very thought-provoking implications for aging. Keeping our energies clean and fresh with positive input — especially high-frequency thoughts, and the nurturing of our physical vessel can only be a benefit. But we must remember that not only are we the caretakers of our own physical, spiritual and energetic bodies, but our actions impact everything and everyone else. As we recognize our power and our vital role as an essential participant in the vast Universal energy ecosystem, we see the impact of our own energy field. Every human has the potential to refresh and vitalize the Universal energy ecology.

THE INFLUENCE — MIND OVER MATTER

In the past fifty years scientists gathered an increasing amount of fascinating data that demonstrates the power of our intent — the power of our will. In quantum mechanics it shows the observer influences the action of an atomic particle. The act of viewing changes the particle's behavior; the observer and the observed are inexorably connected. Scientists are now viewing that phenomenon in a series of experiments that show humans are actually capable of directing their thoughts to impact the environment around them — a true manifestation of mind over matter.

Some of the very early experiments in human interaction with matter date back to the 1930s when Dr. T. Fukauri, a Professor at the Kohyassan University in Japan, demonstrated the ability of a clairvoyant subject to imprint words and pictures on photographic salts by merely holding the thought in her mind. He called the phenomenon "thoughtography." In the 1960s, Dr. Jule Eisenbud, a doctor at the University of Colorado Medical School, had similar and repeatable results with a "sensitive" who was able to project onto film his mental images when holding a Polaroid or TV camera. Around the same time, a nun and chairman of the chemistry department at Rosary Hill College in Brooklyn, NY, Dr. M. Justa Smith, began working with healers seeking to learn if their abilities could be documented scientifically. Smith showed that the energy emitted from the hands of a healer could impact the growth rate of enzymes in a test tube. In the late 1950s, Dr. Bernard Grad at the McGill University in Montreal conducted studies that showed the ability of healers to speed up the healing of open wounds on mice. He also discovered that healers could reduce the growth of cancers. In his studies with plants, McGill found that healers could energize the water that was fed to flora, increasing the chlorophyll.

Hunt began her pioneering studies at UCLA in the early 1970s. Using auric readers of varying disciplines and backgrounds, she demonstrated with bio-sensing equipment that what the readers reported occurring with her subjects had corresponding electromagnetic validity. Furthermore, Hunt was able to verify the transference of energy from the healer to the person being healed and the corresponding change in wavelength of the receiver. In other studies, she was able to document the reaction of a subject's energy field to stimulus prior to any physical sensation. She also linked disruption in the energy field with dysfunction in the body's physical system. And finally, she showed that higher states of consciousness did indeed correlate with high-frequency energy emissions. People whose focus was on their material existence showed lower frequency dispersion.

In the 1970's Dr. Fritz-Albert Popp, theoretical biophysicist at the University of Marburg in Germany, created a machine to measure photons of light radiating from plants, seedlings and eventually people. He noted the high intensity, coherent field demonstrated by healthy subjects and the lack of coherence and dimming light in those that were dying.

Now the studies began to take a leap into new territory. Scientists wanted to know if will or "intent" could influence the outcome of random motion. Could it be statistically proven that a human's intent to change an outcome would actually succeed?

In the same decade Hunt and Popp were doing their experiments, Dr. Helmut Schmidt, a physicist at the Boeing Scientific Research laboratory and later at Rhine Research Institute for Parapsychology, created a machine called a Random Number Generator (RNG.) It electronically generated a random sequence of heads and tails, which would illuminate a circle of lights. Heads moved the light in one direction, tails in the other. The subjects were to concentrate on making the light move clockwise or counterclockwise. Data reveals when left to its own devices the natural split would be half tails, half heads. Schmidt showed that statistically over the course of the study his subjects could influence the movement of the light one way or the other. Interestingly, sometimes he would encounter individuals who actually concentrated on one direction, only to see the light go the opposite direction!

Dr. Robert Jahn and Dr. Brenda Dunne at Princeton University followed with studies in a program called Princeton Engineering Anomalies Research (PEAR). The PEAR machine was called a Random Event Generator (REG), whose randomness came from free electrons bouncing around inside, triggering a sequence that resulted in a selection of 1's and 0's. These experiments tasked participants to concentrate and create more 1's than 0's. After 5,000 trials the results were undeniable: the human mind could influence the outcome. Numerous eminent scientists around the globe performed similar experiments with REG's and came to the same conclusion. Dr. Robert Nelson and Dr. Dean Radin of Princeton crunched the numbers for 800 REG studies by 68 teams, calculating that 51% of the time the subject was able to move the needle. That may not sound like a big distinction, but they ascertained that the odds against that 1% occurring naturally were a trillion to one.

Also in the 1970s, scientists were opening explorations on new fronts. Dr. William Braud, a psychologist at the University of Houston, began using a polygraph to gain insight into whether there would be a physiological response in people who were receiving mental images from others not in their presence. He had one group of participants "stare at" others without their knowledge. Braud observed that his machines showed a corresponding response from those being stared at during the exact moments that his "starers" engaged in their staring exercise.

Meanwhile, Dr. Hal Puthoff and Dr. Russell Targ at the Stanford Research Institute were collaborating on a study of "remote viewing," the ability of one person to receive a mental image from another one sending it from a remote location. This work employed largely gifted "sensitives" and the studies ranged far and wide, varying the circumstances. First they sent "senders" out to locations around the community, and then recorded the impressions of the "receivers." The two doctors then dispatched the senders to remote locations around the world. The results were astonishingly accurate and in fact, some were incorporated in the CIA's first exploration of "remote viewing" as a possible intelligence tactic. Jahn and Dunne at Princeton went one step further in their own follow-up inquiry, asking the "receivers" to provide impressions before the "sender" even arrived at his intended location!

Here's one study that seems to defy belief, documented by Dr. Helmut Schmidt. He used a REG machine to record "clicks" onto a tape that randomly, but evenly, split the "clicks" into left and right sides on a headphone. He locked away the master tape into a vault and verified the 50/50 split on a control tape. He gave the control tape to a volunteer and sent him home with the instruction to influence the "clicks" more to one side of the headphones. Amazingly, his volunteer did just that! On a previously-recorded tape his volunteer somehow changed the past...or perhaps changed the reality.

Dr. Masaru Emoto, a researcher and doctor of alternative medicine in Tokyo, Japan, also began to wonder about the impact man had on his environment through looking at the properties of water. In the 1980s Emoto began freezing water drops to examine and photograph the crystallization. When they originated from a pure, clean water source, the crystals showed lovely symmetrical snowflake patterns. Emoto and his staff began separating drops on different petri dishes and either speaking words of love and kindness, or cursing them with words of hatred before freezing the drops. The first group showered with kind words showed beautiful symmetrical crystals, while the second group was inevitably incoherent and misshapen.

Can words and music have the same impact on plants? A study by a third year biology student at the University of Sussex demonstrated that talking to plants and playing pop music increased their rate of germination.

Clearly, if our thoughts can impact the environment around us, what effect do they have on ourselves and our fellow beings?

A variety of studies at Duke University, San Francisco General Hospital, Mid-American Heart Institute and California Pacific Medical Center validate that intercessory prayer or distance healing works. Each study demonstrated the improvement in a group of patients who were prayed over or sent positive healing thoughts, compared to a control group that were not.

Can we do for ourselves what others can do for us? You bet. Dr. Jeanne Achterberg, Director of Research and Rehabilitation Science at the University of Texas Science Center, conducted a study that asked students to focus on increasing certain blood cell types. Each half of the group was given a different assignment as to the type of cell. When their blood counts were taken, their cell count showed an increase in the specific type of cell they were asked to increase. Dr. O. Carl Simonton, Medical Director at the Cancer Counseling and Research Center in Dallas, TX, revealed a statistical analysis that demonstrated the power of visualization to lengthen the life of cancer victims at the center, decrease cancer reoccurrence and improve the quality of life. Harvard University is currently engaged in two studies to evaluate the effectiveness of guided imagery in patient healing. Dartmouth Medical School and Cleveland Clinic have already introduced guided imagery as part of their care practices.

THE INTERFACE

If we assume that the Zero Point Field (sometimes also called the Akashic Field) — or "The Universe" is the infinite storehouse of information — past, present and possibly future (since quantum mechanics and the Theory of Relativity imply that time may be only a factor in our own reality, but not in the greater enfolded Universe.)

If, then, we also assume that our energy body has the ability to interact with the Zero Point Field through the exchange of energy packets of thought, then this threshold between the two becomes a dynamic revolving door. We send out information and we receive information through this vital portal. If you choose to accept this theory, it goes a long way to explaining a lot of unexplained phenomena. Let's take a peek through the door.

Looking at this model we must assume individuals hold their personal history and memory in their own energy bodies; this can also be made accessible through the interaction with the Zero Point Field.

° ***Sudden Insight and Creativity*** — Many people report the feeling that when they have been at their most creative, they feel as if the information is coming from somewhere else and just flowing through them. This could be accounted for by raising their vibration momentarily to access the Zero Point Field's storehouse of wisdom and knowledge.

○ *Aura Reading, Psychic Reading* — Reader goes into a higher state of consciousness to raise his or her vibration to resonate with and access the Zero Point Field data on the person being read, as well as directly reading the person's energy body.

○ *Channeling* — A channeler (someone who gets messages from those people who have died or other spirits) raises his or her vibration to connect with energy bodies that have already rejoined the Zero Point Field and resonates at a very high level.

○ *Mind Reading* — Reader raises his/her vibration to connect with the subject's energetic field and accesses his or her thoughts.

○ *Psychometry* — The practice of holding someone's object and "reading" their past or present information. The perceiver would be able to read the information from the Zero Point Field by tuning into the resonance of the object and the person being read.

○ *Déjà vu* — The person has a momentary connection with the Zero Point Field, accessing future information that ultimately comes to pass.

○ *Synchronicities* — Individual issues an intention by raising his or her frequency to match the Zero Point Field and sends the message spinning out across the Universe. That thought packet resonates, drawing back the desired or needed information, person or resource.

○ *Ghosts* — This would be the highly charged energy body of the souls who are still riveted to this plane by painful, very grounding memories. They have not been able to raise their vibration level enough to depart.

○ *Remote Viewing* — Receiver resonates through the Zero Point Field to tune into the energy body of the remote sender.

○ *Past Life Experiences* — Re-experiencing past lifetime would be possible because of remnants in this current energy body of memories from past lives. Some experiences travel from lifetime to lifetimes until the memories are addressed and released or otherwise processed.

○ *Phantom Limbs* — Many amputees experience the sense their missing limb still has feeling. This is because the energy in the extremity still exists as it was when it was fully present.

95

° *Memory Re-Experience* — Many times people re-experience pain-ful memories during massage or therapeutic touch. Such memories are embedded in the key *chakras* connected to the energy body. Release can come from touching the corresponding physical point or through addressing the issue in the energetic body.

° *Out-of-Body Experience* — An event or emotion causes the as-tral body — which remains connected to the physical body through what is consistently described as a silver cord — to travel through the Zero Point field to visit the past, present or future. Such discon-nected energy bodies have been known to travel through the Zero Point Field instantly to view scenes — and even numbers — that they can report later.

° *Pre-Natal Memory* — Some people have, under hypnosis or in other higher states of awareness remembered details from the womb or from their mother's viewpoint before birth. Under hypnosis my moth-er described perfectly the hotel room where my grandmother stayed the night before she gave birth. My grandmother never returned to that room after my mother's arrival. This would be possible if the energy field was already at full consciousness.

° *Near-Death Experience* — As death approaches, an individual's soul vibration rapidly increases, (remember that the body's is de-creasing) allowing consciousness to open the door into the Zero Point Field. This would account for why many see their lives "flash before their eyes." When people are called back to their Earthly real-ity, their vibration descends and the energy body returns to earth.

° *Morphic Resonance* — In 1981, biologist Dr. Rupert Sheldrake pro-posed in his book *A New Science of Life* a theory postulating all living organisms are subject to "morphic resonance," a cumulative memory that imposes itself on all of its like species. If one behavior is practiced enough, it gets absorbed into the culture through a process that is not necessarily based on contact. His theory would seem to be borne out by Dr. Lyall Watson, an author and zoology researcher in South Africa, who reported on a study of monkeys who learned a behavior on one island, but shortly thereafter monkeys on an island remote from the original site began to practice the same behavior. This would be possible by information transfer over the Zero Point Field.

○ *Collective Consciousness* — Can human energies united create a "blip" in the vast Universe? That's what Dr. Dean Radin set out to learn when he had three laboratories around the world turn on the Random Event Generators on the day of the reading of the O.J. Simpson verdict. Undoubtedly you recall the huge amount of public frenzy over the case. And yes, the readouts showed peaks at the moment of the trial beginning, the start of the proceedings and the exact moment the verdict was announced. The Universe was listening!

YOUR ENERGY BODY

A person's energy body has three major interconnecting elements. One is the overall aura or capsule of energy that surrounds the body, most often in an oval shape extending 24 to 36 inches outward from the surface of the body. Channels of energy represent the second and connect the seven main energy vortexes or *chakras* regulating energy coming into and going out of the energy body These seven *chakras* reside on the same linear alignment as the body's primary energy meridian, through the center of the body, energetically paralleling the structure and function of the spinal cord to the physical body. Doctors of Oriental Medicine were among the first to recognize the extensive energy pathways, using them for the treatment of illness through acupuncture. The third is the connection with the Universe through the *chakra* system of energy exchange.

The seven *chakras* each correspond with key aspects of our terrestrial and spiritual lives, and the frequency of energy that we hold in them indicates how well we are advancing in our consciousness. As our frequency rises, we clear emotional roadblocks, heal illnesses, and generally become happier, more self-actuated beings.

The first or "root" *chakra* is located at the bottom of our torso or tailbone and is generally seen to have a red color. This *chakra* is associated with physical survival and our physical connection to the Earth and its energy. Socially and emotionally, it is related to matters having to do with how we relate to the external world — family, cultural heritage, community and the world at large. The energy here involves issues of safety, acceptance by society and our place in the world.

The second *chakra* is located near the sexual organs, between the pubic bone and the navel and is generally seen to be orange. This *chakra* is associated with matters related to sex, money, work, creativity, power, vital energy, control and morality. The energy here involves issues of sexuality, our relationship to money and the flow of your inspiration. It is our creative center.

The third *chakra* is called the emotional center and is located in the solar plexus region above the stomach and just below the ribs. It is generally seen to have a pink or yellow color. This *chakra* is the center of emotion and desire and is associated with self-esteem and how you perceive yourself in relationship to others. The energy here involves matters of self-confidence, self-respect, emotional vulnerability to others, sense of honor, fear and ego.

The fourth *chakra* is the heart *chakra* and is generally seen to be green. This *chakra* is a link between the upper and lower chakras. It enables feelings of interconnectedness with all things and therefore enables compassion. This *chakra* is associated with love and forgiveness. The energy here involves matters of love and acceptance, hope, empathy, kindness and commitment. On the other hand this is also the center of hatred, selfishness, anger, grief, bitterness and resentment when it is out of balance.

The fifth *chakra* is in the throat and is generally seen to be blue. This *chakra* is associated with how we express ourselves and communicate, and as such it is associated with sound and its creative expressions. This *chakra* deals with our strength of will, and the energy here involves following one's passion, voicing our feelings and opinions in the world, standing up for oneself, criticizing and judging ourselves and others, and our ability to influence others. This is also the seat of our addictions.

The sixth *chakra* is the site of intuition and insight of which the intellect is one expression. This *chakra* is located on the forehead just above the bridge of the nose and between the eyes. It is often called the "third eye" and is seen to have a gold or indigo color. Besides intuition and insight, intelligence and wisdom, this *chakra* is associated with sight beyond the five senses, plus clarity and soul force. The energy here involves intellectual and Universal truth, ability to grasp the lessons in life, including the purpose and meaning of our emotions, learning to trust intuition and the information available to us, willingness to entertain the opinions of others, questing for greater knowledge and education.

The <u>seventh</u> *chakra* at the top of the head is the spiritual center or "crown" *chakra*, often visualized as the "thousand petalled lotus" as it is known in Buddhism. It is seen generally to be white or violet. This *chakra* is associated with all matters of the spirit. The energy here involves our *chakra* and its connection to the non-physical universe. This is the primary portal for energy entering our *chakra* system. It is associated with man's connection and faith in the Universe, our values and ethics, our selflessness and our desire to help others.

Aura readers report that most of these *chakras* appear like a pinwheel or whirling vortex of energy, extending out from a funnel-like core. These funnels are essentially senders and receivers of energy, pulling energy out of the Universe according to our conscious or unconscious will. Energy can be transported between the *chakras* up and down the midline (meridian) that connects them. Each of the *chakras* is associated with a series of organs, and dysfunction or energy obstruction in a *chakra* can presage illness in the corresponding organ. These *chakras* and their corresponding organs can harbor old memories, including those from past lives, essentially packets of energy information stuck from long ago, which are one of the main sources of blockages to a free flow of life force energy. This is why massage and therapeutic touch can cause the replay of old memories. These memories get repressed and trapped because of their overwhelming emotional charge. Some people actually experience moments of clarity from a past life through touch therapy. Other people may not consciously remember a past life, but the emotional residue from a previous existence can also clog up the energetic works, lodging in the energy body until released.

One method of releasing emotional charges from old memories and past lives is to call forth the memory, examine and lovingly allow it to go. Meditation and deep breathing exercises can help in the process. Or alternatively, the belief enabling the memory's existence can be located, released and replaced with a positive belief or thought that generates a positive reality.

The healthy aura, which is the extended energetic body around each individual, generally has a mix of iridescent colors that reflect the person's vibrant mental, physical and energetic state. However, colors in the *chakras* and the aura change depending on the thoughts, memories and emotional charges held within. Color represents wavelength or frequency of the thought held in that portion of the energy body. Thus, if the person is depressed or angry or driven by fear, the energy visible in the aura will be gray or black and may be incoherent or diffused and muddy in appearance. Uplifting, positive, high-frequency thoughts create luminous colors, oftentimes topped by a brilliant gold, and the aura in that area is generally very coherent and clear. Pink is the color of love and in fact UCLA researcher Dr. Valerie Hunt reported measuring energy frequencies emitted from subjects registering feelings of love as being in the pink range — as she interpreted — blending the vitality of red with the white of higher consciousness.

In consciously managing one's energy the auras and the *chakras* can be a very valuable starting place. Throughout this book, we explore the art of Conscious Creation and the ability to use our imagination to make real what is not to us yet visible. This is the same principle. In working with one's energy, you must use your mind to imagine the energetic system and to give it commands. You are directing energy through your will. What you can envision, you can make reality.

For example, if you wish to replenish your energy supply, imagine a golden cord extending from your root *chakra* at your tailbone down into the Earth. See a golden ball of swirling energy at the end of the cord. Call up the energy from that cord into your body. Now see a similar golden ball above your head and run a cord up to that illuminated light. Allow that light to come down and mix with the other light. You have now performed an act called "grounding," which keeps balance in your energetic system.

Here are a few other examples of how one can use Consciously Creative imagery to help manage vibrational flow in the energetic body:

○ Let's say you want to open your channel to the Universe. See a large cone extending upward from your crown *chakra* opening to receive information from the Universe, and welcome that flow.

° If you want to open your heart to the world, then see your heart opening and sending pink light out far and wide.

° If you want to release anger, pack up those negative wavelengths into a neat tidy balloon, shove the balloon out of your aura, shoot it to the far horizon into the wisdom of the Universe, and watch it just explode into tiny harmless pieces.

° If you want more balance in your life, allow the lovely green color of balance and harmony to wash over you like a waterfall, starting at your crown *chakra* and working its way down.

° If you want to start healing a particular part of your body, assemble those molecules of healing high-frequency light and send them off to mend the energetic blockage. Really feel the radiance of that energy at work in the area.

Energy management of the aura and *chakras* can actually be enjoyable and fun. There are a number of guidebooks on the *chakras* and the aura that can be exceedingly helpful in this process, including: Karla McLaren's *Your Aura and Your Chakras, The Owner's Manual*; Caroline Myss's *Anatomy of the Spirit*; Barbara Y. Martin's *Change Your Aura, Change Your Life*. However, if you begin actively practicing energy management, don't underestimate its power to change your life and prepare to enjoy the benefits of your work.

Scientific Studies in
Human Energy and Consciousness

The following constitute a random look at a series of scientific studies that are anything but random in their conclusions. They are an emerging body of evidence for the physics of consciousness. Three books in particular provide a wealth of information and should be "must" reading for anyone interested in pursuing further knowledge in this fascinating field: Lynne McTaggart's *The Field, The Quest for the Secret Force of the Universe*; Dr. Valerie Hunt's *Infinite Mind, Science of the Human Vibrations of Consciousness*, Michael Talbot's *The Holographic Universe*, and Peter Tompkins and Christopher Bird's *The Secret Life of Plants*. The following summaries — and the previous scientific chronology — are taken from the books cited above and other volumes which are included in the "Recommended Reading" section of this book.

ENERGY IN NATURE

Researcher: Dr. Jacques Benveniste, M.D., University of Paris
Decade: 1980s
Study: Benveniste was seeking to determine if a highly diluted solution of allergens could impact white blood cells. But although he diluted the solution, the impact remained steady on the blood cells. It was if the allergen remained in the solution even though there was no possible remnant of the original molecules. In measuring the solution's properties, he discovered the water carried the energy imprint of the original allergen. It was transferring its properties through resonance.

Researcher: Dr. Harold S. Burr, Neuroanatomist, Yale University
Decade: 1940s
Study: Burr measured electrical fields of plants and animals. Even when a salamander was yet an unfertilized egg, he discovered it has the energy field of an adult. He also documented fully adult plant energy fields around tiny seedlings, yet to begin growing. The strength of the fields was able to accurately predict which seedlings would thrive the most.

Researcher: Dr. Harold S. Burr, Neuroanatomist, Yale University
Decade: 1940s
Study: Burr's study of electrical fields in mold, animals and humans yielded a wealth of information about the impact that different stimuli had on the energy body, including light, water and weather. He also examined the unique patterns that occurred related to growth, sleep, regeneration and cancer.

Researcher: Dr. Robert O. Becker, Orthopedic Surgeon, Director of Orthopedic Surgery at the Veterans Hospital in Syracuse; Professor of Medicine at New York University's Upstate Medical Center
Decade: 1970s
Study: Becker did extensive studies on animals, looking at the mechanism that allows some organisms to regenerate severed body parts. He tracked the electromagnetic energy in salamanders, discovering there was a jolt of increased voltage just before the new limb appeared.

Researcher: Fritz-Albert Popp, Theoretical Biophysicist, University of Marburg, Germany
Decade: 1970s
Study: Popp created a "photomultiplier" machine to read photons or light waves emanating from plants and seedlings. He discovered they emitted a very coherent high-frequency light. Further exploration with animals and humans demonstrated there was a constant level of photon emission until the life force began to decline. Then he viewed a steady decrease in light and coherence.

Researcher: Fritz-Albert Popp, Theoretical Biophysicist, University of Marburg, Germany
Decade: 1970s
Study: Popp wanted to see if there was an energy exchange within a species, so he looked at both water fleas and fish. His findings showed they were each "sucking up" light from their companions. The wave resonance was being used as a communication tool between them. He speculated this may be the way schools of fish and flocks of birds maintain their ordered transit.

Researchers: Dr. Dennis Milner and E. F. Smart, University of Birmingham, England
Decade: 1950s
Study: These two doctors were exploring the electrical charge of plants pressed between two glass plates. They photographed the emanations from the leaves and then removed the leaves. After insuring they had clean, dry plates they discovered pulsating energy globules they interpreted to be the unseen energy of the Universe — the Zero Point Field, in later terminology.

Researcher: Cleve Backster, Polygraph Expert, American Polygraph Association
Decade: 1960s-1970s
Studies: Backster conducted several fascinating studies. He burned the leaf of a plant and using an attached electrode measured the response in the rest of the plant, just as he would have done with a human. He found that the plant signified the same type of stress on the polygraph machine he would have expected had a person suffered the injury. Backster then burned the leaf on a neighboring plant and the original plant registered pain as well.

Researcher: Cleve Backster, Polygraph Expert, American Polygraph Association
Decade: 1960s-1970s
Study: Backster found an array of emotions that plants seem to experience. He discovered that if a plant feels threatened, it reacts in self-defense by "passing out" or going into a deep faint. His plants responded by fainting at the presence of a physiologist whose job it was to kill plants for scientific research. In another case the plants accurately "picked out" the culprit from a "line-up" of candidates who had killed a plant. When one of his guests reported mentally comparing unfavorably Vogel's philodendron to one the guest had at home, Vogel's plant went into a "depression" for almost two weeks.

Researcher: Cleve Backster, Polygraph Expert, American Polygraph Association

Decade: 1960s-1970s

Study: Backster's studies demonstrated that plants bond with their keeper and they can respond wherever he or she may be. Using synchronized stopwatches, he saw the plants "perk up" at the very moment he decided to return home from a trip. He tracked a plant's stressful reaction to the owner's fear while experiencing an airplane landing 700 miles away. He ran numerous experiments that documented plants' physiological response to their owner's emotions and thoughts.

Researcher: Cleve Backster, Polygraph Expert, American Polygraph Association

Decade: 1960s-1970s

Study: His studies demonstrate plants react to the death of other living cells. He first learned this upon cutting his finger and noticing the reaction of the plants to the destruction of the cells. He saw the same reaction again with his plants that he attributed to the death of live bacteria in yogurt when he mixed the yogurt with ingredients killing the live cultures. Backster then deliberately killed brine shrimp by boiling them in water and got a strong reaction from his plants. He demonstrated the same phenomenon with other types of living cells, yeast, mold cultures, blood and sperm among them, determining they — like plants — would also react to the death of fellow living cells.

Researcher: Cleve Backster, Polygraph Expert, American Polygraph Association

Decade: 1960s-1970s

Study: When Backster noticed the plants reacting violently to his cracking open an egg for breakfast, he decided to test an egg itself. He was astounded to see that his equipment gave him a reading corresponding to the rhythm of the heartbeats of a chicken embryo about three to four days along in incubation. Except that the egg was store-bought, had never been fertilized, nor could he find any physical circulatory structure to account for the pulsation.

Researcher: S.P. Shchurin, Institute of Automation and Electrometry, Russia
Decade: 1970s
Study: The study involved placing two vials of identical tissue cultures near each other, but separated initially by a wall of glass. They deliberately killed the colony of cells in one vial and the other one continued to thrive. Then they repeated the experiment by putting a wall of quartz between the two, and not only did the cells in the poison-injected vessel die, but so did those untouched cells on the other side of the quartz wall. They concluded that since ultraviolet waves cannot pass through glass, but can pass through quartz, the cells were communicating through ultraviolet energy.

Researcher: George De La War, Civil Engineer, and Marjorie De La War,
Osteopath, England
Decade: 1950s
Study: The De La Wars wanted to determine if a rooting taken from a "mother" plant would thrive when separated, but still "connected" energetically to its parent. Rootings did fine, until the "mother" plant was destroyed. Those with still living "mother" plants continued to grow heartily. Further studies produced the same results when the "mothers" and offshoots were separated by hundreds of miles.

Researcher: Vladimir Grigorievich Karmanov, Director of the Laboratory of
Biocybernetics of the Institute of Agrophysics, Russia
Decade: 1950s-60s
Study: Using sophisticated sensors, Karmanov found that navy bean plants were able to signal their desire for water and to regulate themselves for two-minute drinks each hour. The same plants could indicate how long a day/night cycle they wanted, whether the plant was too hot or cold, and when it wanted nutrients.

Researcher: Sir Jagadis Chandra Bose, Institute of Research, India
Decade: 1900s
Study: Bose recognized that minerals produced radio waves resembling those omitted by muscles. When exertion "fatigued" the minerals, a gentle massage

or a warm bath of water renewed their radio waves to health. Some minerals responded strongly to other substances repellant to them, creating the same reaction muscular tissue demonstrates when exposed to poison.

EVIDENCE OF THE ENERGY BODY AND ITS POWER TO HEAL

Researchers: Valentina and Seymon Kirlian, Russia
Decade: 1940-50s
Study: This couple became famous for their "Kirlian Photos," the result of years of photographing objects and people with the apparatus they devised for capturing high-frequency, high-voltage, low-current, electrical luminescence. In 1949 they conducted one study of twin leaves from different plants of the same species. They noticed a great distinction between the two in the photos and wondered why. They subsequently learned that the one leaf came from a plant that was diseased, though the leaf did not show it yet physically. By capturing its energy signature they were able to project or diagnose the leaf's impending illness.

Researchers: Valentina and Seymon Kirlian, Russia
Decade: 1940-50s
Study: In this study, the Kirlians cut away a portion of a leaf before taking the photograph. The resulting image showed a whole energy body, complete even where the leaf had been excised.

Researcher: Dr. M. Justa Smith, Biochemist, Chairman of the Chemistry Department, Rosary Hill College Buffalo, NY
Decade: 1950s
Study: Sister Smith (she was also a nun) documented that emanations from the hands of a proven healer could positively affect the growth rate of enzymes in a test tube.

Researcher: Dr. Bernard Grad, Associate Professor of Gerontology, McGill University, Montreal
Decade: 1950s
Study: Grad set up experiments to test whether the energy from healers' hands could impact the open wounds in mice. In fact, he found they could not only markedly speed the healing in the mice, but also reduce the growth of cancers.

Researcher: Dr. Bernard Grad, Associate Professor of Gerontology, McGill University, Montreal
Decade: 1950s
Study: Grad had a healer treat the water that was fed to half the number of plants in the study. The plants receiving the energized water showed a distinctive increase in chlorophyll.

Researcher: Dr Doris Kreiger, Professor of Nursing, New York University.
Decade: 1970s
Study: Kreiger conducted multiple studies in the impact of therapeutic touch on hemoglobin. One study included 64 patients, half of which were treated with therapeutic touch. The trained therapists drew information from the patients' electromagnetic field and then directed their energies to where they and the patient perceived an imbalance. No changes in the 32 members of the control group were found, but all 32 in the treated group showed measured improvement in their hemoglobin statistics.

Researcher: Dr. Elmer Green, Biophysiology, Menninger Clinic, Topeka, KS
Decade, 1990s
Study: Green originated the concept of clinical biofeedback. In his studies he looked at the energy emissions of healers and non-healers in a meditative state. He found that healers far surpassed the electromagnetic energy dispensed by the non-healers.

Researcher: Dr. Jacques Benveniste, M.D., University of Paris
Decade: 1980s
Study: Benveniste was among the first to demonstrate that cell communication operated on a frequency wavelength, and that each molecule and atom in the body had its own unique frequency.

Researcher: Dr. Valerie Hunt, Psychologist and Physiologist, University of California Los Angeles
Decade: 1970s
Study: Hunt used sensitive electromagnetic detection equipment to record electrical activity during a treatment by a modern shamanic healer on a subject. During her study, she taped the comments of a sensitive or aura reader who could see both auras. In reviewing the readout of her equipment, she observed a direct correlation between what the reader saw and what the instruments noted in terms of timing and color frequency range. The data showed an increase in amplitude in the region where the reader said energy was flowing. In one case the reader reported seeing energy that had been plugging up the heart *chakra* suddenly released, and spurting up through the crown *chakra*. Indeed, Hunt's equipment showed a sudden burst of energy coming from the electrodes at the top of the head.

Researcher: Dr. Valerie Hunt, Psychologist and Physiologist, University of California Los Angeles
Decade: 1970s
Study: Hunt used a telemetry system designed originally for NASA to measure, intercept and project the body's electrical activity. Her studies began with dancers who were receiving Rolfing treatments, a technique akin to deep tissue massage, but that actually separates and stretches the connective tissue. While the treatments were ongoing, Hunt had known aura readers report what they were seeing, the movement of energy in and out of *chakra* centers and the colors that were visible. Hunt's equipment readouts showed direct correlation between the aura readers reportage and energy dispersion within the dancer's bodies. The frequency of the energy corresponded directly to specific color wavelengths seen by the aura reader. Hunt documented the transfer

of energy from the Rolfer to the subject. She saw that when a dancer was in a higher state of consciousness or reported imaging, the Rolfer's hands were white; if the subject expressed pain, the Rolfer's hands changed to violet-pink, the color of peace and calming, which indeed seemed to have that effect.

Researcher: Dr. Valerie Hunt, Psychologist and Physiologist, University of California Los Angeles
Decade: 1970s
Study: Hunt set out to learn whether the energy field "sensed" something before the human body was even aware of it. Using various forms of stimuli, including light, sound, touch and environmental vibrations, her lab assistants stroked the subject's aura with a feather while the person was blindfolded, varied the intensity of light vibrations, created sounds above and below the known range of hearing. Each time the person's field responded in frequency readings before there was increased brain activity or physical feeling.

Researcher: Dr. Valerie Hunt, Psychologist and Physiologist, University of California Los Angeles
Decade: 1970s
Study: Hunt continued to document the transfer of energy from healers to those being healed. Initially as the healing began, her data indicated there was a differentiation between the frequency readings of both parties. When a healing was completed, however, the fields of the healer and the subject showed an identical pattern.

Researcher: Dr. Valerie Hunt, Psychologist and Physiologist, University of California Los Angeles
Decade: 1970s
Study: Hunt wanted to see how changing any of the properties of electro-magnetic energy in a person's environment would impact both the individual and their energy body. She then set up her equipment, invited an aura reader to observe and isolated a variety of subjects in a Mu Room. This is a laboratory in the university's physics department where natural electromagnetic energy could be changed without altering the level of gravity or oxygen content. Her

subjects were asked to perform balance and dance movements as the scientists raised and lowered the electrical and magnetic aspects within the room.

When the electrical aspect of the atmosphere in the room was withdrawn, the auric fields became randomly disorganized, scattered and incoherent. The subjects became so disoriented they were completely unaware of the location of their bodies in space. Interestingly, the aura reader also reported a dispersed energy in a fishnet pattern that no longer behaved as it would normally (a coherent pattern flowing along the meridian pathways.) The subjects' emotional balance was also impacted, some bursting into tears. When the field was re-established to normal balance, all sensory and energetic systems returned to status quo. However, when the scientists increased the electrical aspect above normal, the subjects reported great mental clarity and expansion of consciousness. Correspondingly, the aura readers saw auras radiating white light. When the experiment was reoriented around the magnetism in the room, it seemed to impact balance and coordination. A waning magnetic environment resulted in a lack of coordination, and once restored, the subjects recovered their balance and motor coordination. Hunt concluded that for all physical systems to work, a complete electromagnetic field had to be present in the environment.

Researcher: Dr. Valerie Hunt, Psychologist and Physiologist, University of California Los Angeles
Decade: 1970s
Study: Hunt conducted an experiment with subjects lying with the soles of their feet connected. Again she employed aura readers and her equipment to document any energy transfer. On one occasion a reader saw a large sudden pulse of energy in the leg of one of the subjects. A moment later, the second subject experienced an extreme muscle spasm.

Researcher: Dr. Valerie Hunt, Psychologist and Physiologist, University of California Los Angeles
Decade: 1970s
Study: Hunt set out to compare how the energy system corresponded to physical conditions. She took measurements of patients with dysrhythmic

heart ailments. She discovered the energy field around the patient showed a non-coherent, out-of-sync energy pattern. Comparing the heart patterns and energy patterns, she found them to be virtually the same. In comparison a study of healthy hearts revealed a coherent and rhythmic pattern in the energy field.

Researcher: Dr. Valerie Hunt, Psychologist and Physiologist, University of California Los Angeles
Decade: 1970s
Studies: Many of Hunt's various studies discerned one consistent finding: If the individual's energy field achieved the highest vibrations through imaging, meditation, self-hypnosis or other means, that individual reported supreme spiritual experiences — the sense of oneness with the Universe, a profound sense of love and peace, a great "knowing" and so forth. Regardless of the subject's religious orientation or cultural background, the experiences all showed the common denominator of a sense of connecting with a higher power.

Researcher: Dr. Valerie Hunt, Psychologist and Physiologist, University of California Los Angeles
Decade: 1970s
Study: Though not a major focus of study, one of the more unique findings was that a person's energy system showed higher vibrations after having been in the mountains, near the sea, in a pool, or having had a shower. Such activities enhanced and expanded the person's aura.

POWER OF THOUGHTS

Researcher: Dr. T. Fukurai, Professor, Kohyassan University, Japan
Decade: 1930s
Study: Fukurai asked a young clairvoyant to concentrate on transferring her mental images of Japanese words and letters to the silver salts on a photographic plate. She was in fact able to repeatedly achieve the feat.

Researcher: Dr. Jule Eisenbud M.D., Psychiatrist, Psychoanalyst, University of Colorado Medical School, Denver
Decade: 1960s
Study: Eisenbud worked with a psychic who was asked to create images on film using thought-transfer, while holding a Polaroid or TV camera. Eisenbud documented his subject's consistent ability to perform this task.

Researchers: Dr. J.B. Rhine, Biologist, and Dr. William McDougall, Chairman of the Department of Psychology, Duke University, North Carolina
Decade: 1920s-1960s
Study: Rhine's study tested a subject's ability to intuit one of five symbols on cards — a cross, star, wavy lines, circle and square. Five correct guesses would be the expected number according to chance. In his initial study of 2,400 total guesses, his subjects had 489 correct responses. Over the course of 33 experiments, encompassing a million trials, 27 studies proved statistically significant. Some of these featured sending and receiving information from one party to another over long or short distances, as well as anticipating the correct symbol before it was selected by the sending party.

Researcher: Dr. J.B. Rhine, Biologist Chairman of the Department of Psychology, Duke University, North Carolina
Decade: 1920s-1960s
Study: Rhine wanted to know if an individual could influence the role of dice. Subjects were asked to pre-specify what number would turn up on a die or set of dice and encouraged to "will" that number to appear. If the number matched the actual rolled dice a "hit" was recorded. The numbers of hits were statistically significant.

Researcher: Karl Pribram, Neurosurgeon, Yale University
Decade: 1970s
Study: Looking to explore brain function, Pribram trained monkeys to respond by pressing a specific lever when they saw a certain card with a swirl, bar or stripes. He planted electrodes in the monkey's visual cortex to register

brainwaves. What interested Pribram most about the study was the monkeys' intention to press the bar was registered before they actually did.

Researcher: Dr. Helmut Schmidt, Research Physicist, Boeing Scientific Research Laboratories
Decade: 1970s
Study: Schmidt created a Random Number Generator (RNG) that electronically generated a random sequence of heads and tails. The apparatus featured a circle of lights responding to each prompt, a "tail" moved the light one direction and a "head" moved it in the opposite. Without interference from any stimulus, the machine would wander back and forth, ultimately splitting the movements in half so that the light would come back to the center point. Schmidt asked subjects to focus their thoughts on moving the light clockwise or counterclockwise, thus changing the number of heads or tails. This would impose order on the randomness. To conduct the experiments, he chose psychics and other "sensitives" who had demonstrated extrasensory abilities. Schmidt's study showed that his subjects had a demonstrative and statistically reliable ability to move the light. However, an interesting phenomenon was revealed…some of his participants had results opposite to what they were intending to do. The more they concentrated on moving the light one way, the more it would go the opposite direction.

Researchers: Dr. Robert Jahn and Dr. Brenda Dunne, Princeton University
Decade: 1970s-1990s
Study: Jahn and Dunne wanted to know if the "average" person could have the same impact as the psychically gifted ones in Schmidt's studies. The two researchers created a variation of the RNG called a Random Event Generator (REG) at their lab, calling the resulting study the Princeton Engineering Anomalies Research (PEAR.) The REG produced random 1's and 0's by catching the free electrons bouncing around the system. By nature the REG would register an equal number of 1's and 0's when a button was pressed to start the sequence. Subjects were instructed to press the button and then focus on generating more of one over the other. Each individual performed the test 50 to 100 times. The results after 5,000 studies showed pronounced

deviation from the medium. In further studies over the course of 12 years and 2.5 millions trials, the results demonstrated that 52 percent of all the attempts were in the intended direction. More than 60 percent of the subjects had success in influencing the machines the way they desired.

Researchers: Dr. Robert Jahn and Dr. Brenda Dunne, Princeton University
Decade: 1970s-1990s
Study: The Princeton team developed a pinball-like device that allowed 9,000 three-quarter inch marbles to circulate around 330 nylon pegs, sorting into 19 bins at the bottom. Generally, without influence, more balls would fall in the center than the outsides, creating a bell curve. Participants were asked to put more marbles into the outer bins. After concluding the study, there was further evidence that the mind could influence matter as the subjects were generally able to re-distribute the balls to where they were directed.

Researchers: Dr. Roger Nelson and Dr. Dean Radin, Princeton University
Decade: 2000's
Study: Nelson and Radin chose to combine the results of the 800 REG experiments conducted by 68 individual investigating teams into one massive statistical analysis. 51% of the time the subject was able to move the needle, and calculated the odds of this happening naturally were a trillion to one.

Researchers: Dr. Montague Ullman, Albert Einstein College of Medicine, Founder of Maimonides Medical Center, Brooklyn and Dr. Stanley Krippner
Decade: 1960s
Study: The Maimonides Medical Center, well known for its Dream Research Laboratory, sponsored research into many different aspects of dreaming. A particular study of interest directed one party to look at a picture, painting or other vision and concentrate on it. Then another sleeping subject in a different locality would be awakened and asked to report his or her dreams. The dreamer more often than not had very specific images that correlated with the "sending" party's visual experience. Statistics showed this accuracy rate to be 84%.

Researcher: Dr. William Braud, University of Houston
Decade: 1970s
Studies: Braud conducted studies where one person was held in the mind of another while in separate rooms. In some of these cases, the object of the study was being stared at and in other situations he or she was being sent positive messages. Braud used a polygraph, which measured the response of the energy radiating from the skin, to see if the object of the experiment registered a response at the moment he/she was being held in the mind of the sender. Braud was able to correlate a direct response in the person who was the object and, in fact, concluded getting positive energy or thoughts from another was just as effective as receiving one's own positive biofeedback.

Researcher: Dr. William Braud, University of Houston
Decade: 1970s
Studies: In another study Braud asked some participants to direct their minds to disrupting the normal electromagnetic field around a second group, seeking to raise the second group's polygraph response. Others were then instructed to create a mental shield against this effort. A control group was told not to resist or prevent the disruption attempt. Braud found the shielded group showed far fewer physical effects than those in the control group.

Researchers: Dr. Hal Puthoff and Dr. Russell Targ, Stanford Research Institute
Decade: 1970s
Study: These two pioneered studies in "remote viewing," primarily using psychically gifted subjects. Puthoff and Targ directed one party to go out to a location on campus, then across town and ultimately around the world and "send" back the picture of what he/she was viewing to another individual sitting in the lab. The subject in the lab would then report his/her impressions — sometimes as the pictures were being projected, other times after the "sender" left the location. The number of direct "hits" calculated was astonishing to the researchers. Some of the studies became part of the CIA's most extensive look into the value of remote viewing for use as an intelligence-gathering tool.

In fact, the remote viewers were able to provide detailed descriptions of top-secret U.S. and Soviet military installations unknown to them.

Researchers: Dr. Robert Jahn and Dr. Brenda Dunne, Princeton University
Decade: 1980s
Studies: This pair followed up on the Puthoff-Targ study by asking the "receiver" to record impressions *before* the sender arrived at the location…as far in advance as five days. Again, the statistical results were impressive.

Researcher: Stephan A. Schwartz
Decade: 1970s-1980s
Studies: Schwartz successfully used "remote viewers" to pinpoint specific localities where archeologists and researchers would find the remains of various structures, ships and objects on the ocean floor. Initially, in 1979-1980 his team of remote viewers located key archeological sites for the submerged ancient city of Alexandria. In 1985-86 he went looking for Columbus' last two caravels, likely sunk in St. Ann's Bay in Jamaica. In the case of the Caravel Project, the eight remote viewers zeroed in on a specific area, describing the topography, objects, shapes, materials and other specifics. The research and recovery team was able to corroborate a great many of their findings. In the areas they were able to evaluate, the recovery team was able to confirm a "hit rate" of between 57 and 89 percent for the eight viewers, averaging in the high 70 percentile.

Researcher: Dr. Dean Radin, University of Nevada, Las Vegas
Decade: 1990s
Study: Radin created a study where a computer would randomly display color photos of peaceful nature scenes or pictures designed to shock or titillate. Electromagnetic readings from skin, plus heart rate and blood pressure were monitored as the participants viewed the images. As would be expected, the monitors showed that the individuals relaxed while looking at the nature photos and became distressed or aroused at the other ones. However, Radin also discovered that his subjects *anticipated* what they were about to see, registering a response before they had seen the images.

Researcher: Dr. Helmut Schmidt, Boeing Scientific Research Laboratories
Decade: 1980s
Study: Schmidt used a modified REG machine connected to an audio device to record the random distribution of "clicks" that could be heard in the right and left side of a pair of headphones. He did this in a clean environment without being present to ensure that he had no impact on the outcome. Then he stored the master in a vault and counted the clicks on a control tape to make sure they were evenly divided. Next, he asked a volunteer to take the tape home and "will" more clicks to one side over the other. When the tape was returned, the volunteer had indeed succeeded in changing the balance of the clicks on a tape that had been recorded in the past.

Researcher: Dr. Masaru Emoto, International Hado Membership (I.H.M.)
Corporation, Japan
Decade: 1980s
Study: Emoto wanted to research the properties of pure water and water under stress. He placed drops of water in petri dishes, freezing them for two hours before extracting them to be photographed at 200-500 times magnification. Photographs of crystals from clean water had beautiful snowflake patterns. But over the course of five years, Emoto subjected many of the water drops to verbal abuse and messages of anger and hate, while others were given words of love, joy and happiness. When he and his staff placed the frozen crystals under the microscope, they were astounded to find invariably the abused crystals were misshapen or incoherent, while those receiving kind words and love were beautifully formed.

Researchers: Ruth Davies and Dr. Peter Scott, University of Sussex, England
Decade: 2000s
Study: Davies, a third-year graduate student, looked at measuring the germination rates of a variety of plants, including: wallflowers, busy lizzies, basil, phlox, penstemons, maize, tobacco, carrots, cress and mung beans. She tested normal germination rates against plants that were exposed to silence, pop music, rock music, classical music and speech. Both speech and pop music

substantially increased germination. Loud rock music encouraged the wall-flower seeds to sprout two days earlier than those in silent conditions.

Researcher: T.C. Singh, Director Department of Botany, Annamali University, India
Decade: 1950s-1960s
Study: Singh had an associate play traditional Indian music on a stringed instrument to balsam plants. After five weeks the serenaded plants produced an average of 72 percent more leaves than control plants and had grown 20 percent higher. He then had recorded music played to rice paddies growing in the fields of seven villages. The harvests ranged from 25 to 60% higher than the regional average. He got the same results with peanuts and tobacco. He determined in his studies that plants are energized to synthesize greater quantities of food during the period of stimulation, leading to greater yields.

Researchers: George De La War, Civil Engineer, and Marjorie De La War, Osteopath, England
Decade: 1950s
Study: The De La Wars had assistants plant oat seedlings. Half of the assistants were told they were planting the seedlings in irradiated vermiculite-rich soil to increase energy potency, and the other half were told they were using untreated soil. In truth the De La Wars used no treated soil. However, those seedlings tended by the assistants who BELIEVED they were using treated soil came up markedly faster than those tended by the other assistants.

Researcher: Reverend Franklin Loehr, Religious Research Foundation
Decade: 1950s
Study: Seven hundred experiments on the effect of prayer on plants, conducted by 150 persons, using 27,000 seeds showed that the growth rate of plants could be accelerated by as much as 20 percent when individuals or groups visualized plants thriving under ideal conditions.

Researcher: Dr. John Pierrakos, Psychiatrist, New York
Decade: 1970s
Study: Pierrakos can see auras around humans, plants and animals. He subjected plants to the ravings, screaming and emotional outbursts of disturbed patients. He had plants hooked to a monitor and found that a chrysanthemum's field contracts when a person shouts at it from five feet, while its pulsation diminishes by a third. Other plants had their lower leaves drop off and the plants withered and died within three days after abuse.

Researcher: Marcel Vogel, Research Chemist, IBM
Decade: 1960s
Study: Vogel chose to document a plant's specific reactions to human emotions. He observed the death of plants that were being ignored, while others side-by-side were being praised. He went on television with a plant hooked to a galvanometer, illustrating the plant's response to his various emotional states, including his "quieting" of the plant after Vogel's sudden rush of emotion.

Researcher: V.N. Pushkin, Doctor of Psychological Sciences and V.M. Fetisov,
Russia
Decade: 1970s
Study: The two researchers hypnotized a young woman and first implanted the thought that she was the most beautiful woman in the world, then freezing in cold weather and afterwards a variety of other scenarios. A plant was hooked up to an encephalograph nearby. With each change of emotion the girl experienced, the plant registered an appropriate response.

PRAYER, DISTANCE AND SELF-HEALING

Researchers: Dr. Elizabeth Targ, Psychiatrist and Fred Sicher Psychologist,
California Pacific Medical Center's Complementary Research Unit
Decade: 1990s
Study: Targ and Sicher's study was one of the first scientifically-sound research studies designed to look at whether distance "prayer" or positive heal-

ing messages would have an impact on patients. They selected subjects from a pool of AIDS patients and carefully matched them according to their T-cell counts, number of AIDS-defined diseases and so forth. This group was divided into two. One group received the attention of the healers, who were operating remotely. The healers came from 40 different disciplines — spiritual, religious, psychics, aura readers, shaman, etc. Each healer was provided only a photo, a name and a T-cell count. They were asked to hold the intention for health and well-being of the patient for an hour a day, six days a week, for 10 weeks, with alternate weeks off for rest. The healers rotated patient profiles each week to make sure that each patient in the group received the benefit of multiple practitioners. When the study was concluded, Targ realized that all the end-stage AIDS patients who had been the subjects of the healers' attentions were improving. During the six months of the trial, 40% of the control group died, but all of the patients in the healing group were still alive and furthermore, had become much healthier based on medical evaluations. They had less doctor visits, fewer hospitalizations, less days in the hospital, reduced number of illnesses, and the problems were less severe.

Researcher: Dr. Randolph Byrd, Cardiologist, University of California and San Francisco General Hospital
Decade: 1980s
Study: Byrd conducted a 10-month double blind study of 393 patients in the hospital's Coronary Care Unit. In this program they were divided in half, with one group receiving intercessory prayer and the other receiving no special attention beyond normal medical care. The members of the group receiving the ministrations of long-distance prayer had far fewer complications and were significantly healthier.

Researchers: William S. Harris MD, Mid American Heart Institute
Decade: 1990s
Study: This study was very similar to the one conducted at San Francisco General. It looked at hospitalized cardiac patients over the course of 12 months. Those who had the benefit of prayer had a 10% reduction in symptoms.

Researchers: Dr. Mitch Krucoff, Cardiologist, Duke University and Suzanne Crater
Decade: 1990s
Study: Krucoff picked 150 patients with acute coronary problems at the Durham Veterans Affairs Medical Center. Prior to a procedure, half of the patients were treated with guided imagery, stress relaxation, healing touch or intercessory prayer, while the others received no special therapeutic regime. The study showed that the treated group had lower complication rates and lower incidences of post-procedure problems during hospitalization. Those receiving prayer appeared to fare better than those receiving the other types of non-traditional treatments.

Researcher: Dr. O. Carl Simonton, Radiation Oncologist, Medical Director Cancer Counseling and Research Center, Dallas, TX
Decade: 1970s-1980s
Study: Simonton selected patients who had been diagnosed with generally *fatal* cancers and directed them to use visualization to imagine their radiation treatments as tiny bullets attacking their cancer cells with their white cells arriving to carry away the dead cells. Among the 159 patients, the average survival time was 24.4 months, more than twice the national average. Four years later, 63 were still alive, 12 were in remission, 17 were stable and 14 had been cured!

Researcher: Dr. Jeanne Achterberg, Director of Research and Rehabilitation Science, University of Texas Health Science Center, Dallas
Decade: 1980s
Study: Achterberg involved college students in a trial that split them into two groups, asking them to specifically imagine increasing the number of white cells in their bodies. One group was assigned to focus on a type known as neutrophils and the other T-cells. At the end of the study period, their blood counts showed a significant increase in the specific type of cells that they were asked to envision.

Researchers: Dr. S.J. Page, Dr. P. Levine, Dr. S. Sisto and Dr. MV Johnson, Kessler Medical Rehabilitation Research and Education Corporation, Orange, NJ
Decade: 2000s
Study: The program involved patients who had suffered strokes and received physical therapy three times a week. In a random controlled study the group was divided between those who were simply offered stroke information and the remainder who participated in guided imagery sessions. At the conclusion of the study, the patients who were given information showed no change, but those who had been lead in guided imagery had significant improvement in motor recovery based on two numerically scaled systems.

OTHER PHENOMENON

Researcher: Dr. Ian Stevenson, University of Virginia Medical School
Decade: 1960s-1970s
Study: Stevenson conducted interviews with 2,000 children around the world who recalled past life experiences. They produced names and places from perceived past lives very accurately and described their experiences in vivid images. When checking their experiences against the specific facts, Stevenson found that with the children who reported very recent previous lives, 90% of the data was verifiable.

Researcher: Dr Paul Pearsall, Clinical Professor of Psychology, University of Hawaii
Decade: 1990s-2000
In his book, *The Heart's Code: Tapping the Wisdom and Power of our Heart Energy* Pearsall describes transplant patients who receive an organ from another person's body and what he calls their "cellular memories." Recipients have reported inheriting everything from the donor's food cravings to knowledge about his murderer — information that in one case led to the killer's arrest.

Researcher: Dr. Janusz Slawinski, Dept. of Physical Chemistry, Poznan University of Technology, Poland
Decade: 2000
Study: Slawinski studied electromagnetic radiation emanating from dying patients. He reported that a flash of high energy occurs at death, 10 to 1,000 times stronger than the person's normal light emission. He also found there was less radiance from someone who had suffered a long slow decline than one who had a sudden traumatic death.

Researchers: Dr. Karlis Osis and Dr. Janet Lee Mitchell, American Society for Psychical Research, New York
Decade: 1960s-1970s
Study: The researchers asked 100 subjects who consistently manifest out-of-body experiences to report from their homes what objects they were "seeing" in the organization's offices. Of these, 15% were successful, but with similar experiments involving one particular clairvoyant, they found he was correct on eight out of eight occasions.

Researcher: Dr. Dean Radin
Decade: 1990s
Study: Radin and his colleagues wanted to test the theory the moon influenced the intuitive power of individuals and decided there was no better way to do that than review the winnings of casino gamblers during the moon phases. They were provided records of casino payouts and analyzed the results, discovering the peak average payout rate for blackjack occurred consistently three days before the full moon, for craps three days after the full moon and for roulette one day before the full moon.

COLLECTIVE CONSCIOUSNESS

Researcher: Dr. Lyall Watson, Botanist, Zoologist, Biologist, Anthropologist, Ethologist Author & BBC Producer, South Africa

Decade: 1950s

Study: In his book *Lifetide,* Watson reported a Japanese study of monkeys who were learning a new behavior on one island. Thereafter, monkeys on an entirely different island began to practice the same behavior with no visible or logical means of communication. The research gave rise to what Watson termed the "Hundredth Monkey Principle" that says that after a certain number of species learn a behavior it somehow becomes accessible to others who are totally unconnected.

Researcher: Dr. Dean Radin

Decade: 1990s

Study: Radin wanted to test whether an event of mass conscious awareness and focus could move the meters on the sensitive REG computers. He set up five REG computers at three different locations around the world, including the PEAR Lab at Princeton, the University of Amsterdam and the University of Nevada, to determine if they could register the high emotional context of the O.J. Simpson verdict in the global consciousness. And indeed the machines showed peaks when the news coverage began, at the beginning of the courtroom proceedings and most significantly at the moment the verdict was being read. Radin did similar experiments with the 1996 Super Bowl, the 1995 Academy Awards telecast and several other specific events.

VISION POWER:
The CREATION, CARE *and* FEEDING *of* YOUR VISION

Now we know and acknowledge just how powerful we are! As creative visionaries we can learn some very simple steps that will propel our world-healing wishes into the future, calling forth our visions or changing them from probabilities to realities. It's an easy formula, one that can be enhanced, augmented and personalized to fit your lifestyle and preferences.

As our planet wakes up to the mission calling us forth, you will find many opportunities to join with others in group visioning. (More on this in Chapter Eight.) This is fun, fulfilling and invigorating. Feeling the power of others around you will help attune and raise your frequency and will strengthen your sense of purpose. Visionary leaders can help the group achieve a singular focus, increasing the intensity of the message.

Alone, however, you *can still* have significant impact by hitching *your* vision on to the collective consciousness, helping to create the shift. Whereas we can't always find a group to share our vision, we can spare a few minutes a day. First we manifest our personal prospects, then focus on the planetary future.

ENVIRONMENT

The best way to begin is to find a quiet place where you will not be disturbed. Turn off the cell phone, unplug the landline, lock the door, or go outside where you can only hear the birds. Being near the sound of running water is very soothing and can be a real asset in visioning. Water is a conductor of energetic messages. Just find some place that you consider *your* sanctuary.

Find a sitting or lying position where you are most comfortable: sitting in a chair, cross-legged on the floor or lying on a blanket outside in the grass. Just don't get so comfortable that you fall asleep!

You may choose to have "accessories" – crystals, candles, incense or music. Quartz crystals for instance intensify your energy, while other minerals radiate different beneficial vibrations. I like to work with mineral spheres because their symmetry appeals to me and are reminiscent of the earth. There are a number of good guidebooks describing the healing properties of minerals if you'd like to evaluate other stones that might inspire you in this process. Candles are great to help focus your attention on the present moment, but they also serve to accelerate the acceptance and response to your intention. The flame serves as an energy attractor. The lovely scent of incense helps quiet the active mind, allowing the high-frequency, creative mind to come forth. Gentle music has the same effect. But you can do fine without any of these. Silence really is golden in this case.

CALLING FORTH YOUR ENERGY

Close your eyes. Begin by breathing deeply. Do not underestimate this important step. Deep, rhythmic breathing has many benefits in this process. Conscious breathing focuses a person on his or her inner core. It relaxes the body and the mind. The act of breathing helps create resonance and coherence, awakens self-healing and opens the creative portal. It's an act of harmony and balance. Concentrate for a few minutes on feeling the breath go in, permeating your lungs and finding its home in your diaphragm. Then slowly release it.

Let's begin now visualizing your energy. Imagine that you are a beautiful, glowing and translucent cloud of energy that gently conforms to your real shape — just a bit larger. You're ready for your fill-up! Let's ground your energy first by imagining a golden cord from the base of your spine that descends into the earth and connects to the earth's beautiful golden pool of energy. Up through the cord comes new "renewable energy" that meshes with your own. Now imagine opening a funnel, extending upward from your crown *chakra*, allowing golden light to flow downward to you. You are the central meeting place of all this glittering positive light. Let it circulate, filling up all the cells and molecules — feel them responding — refreshing your energy body. Extend this golden light out to the edge of your expanded energy body.

Take your imaginary hand brush now and clean away any residue or negative energies from each of your seven main *chakras* — root *chakra* at the base of your spine; sacral *chakra* just below your bellybutton; third *chakra* or "power center" in the solar plexus area; fourth heart *chakra*; fifth throat *chakra*; sixth *chakra* — also called the 'third eye' which is above the bridge of the nose and between your eyes at the center of your forehead; and the seventh or crown *chakra* at the top of your head. Release any regrets, guilt, pain, fear and worries. Just choose to let them go. Forgive anyone with whom you are angry, because if you don't, it will only weaken your energy. Now let in the love. Imagine beautiful pink light descending to you through the crown *chakra* funnel and pouring over you in waves, or a waterfall, expanding out to the edges of your aura.

Determine if there is any other light you would like to call forth today. Green for balance and healing, purple for peace, lavender for serenity, light blue for inspiration, vivid blue for artistry, silver for perception, gold for wisdom and courage, orange for vitality and motivation, red for energy and passion, or white for purification and protection. You are seeking to re-calibrate your own energy bank by adding the frequencies that will help you function optimally both in the "explicate" world and as a creator in the "implicate" world.

Now think of yourself as resonating with the Universe. Go ahead and light up those little molecules! You're just a fabulous energy being all charged and ready to go.

CREATING AND STRUCTURING YOUR VISION

Each vision is like a finely-crafted movie. It should have an opening, a story (or image) and then an ending. First you decide what your "movie" is going to be. What is it that you want to ask the Universe to create or change? You may want to sit down, think this over or even put it in writing, just to fine-tune it and make it crystal-clear. In the succeeding chapters of this book you will find general outlines of visions for covering a variety of issues as a good starting point. You will want to be very clear and specific about your desires. There's no need to be limited in your vision. Shoot for the stars! Remember that whatever you wish already exists in the "implicate" Universe. We are simply providing the energy to propel it forward into this world. In crafting your vision you need to follow these key steps:

- Focus on what you want to see happen, not what you "don't want."

- Always picture the world, yourself, whatever you are visioning as you wish it to be.

- Choose a positive focus — not one that blames or condemns. You must operate from a framework of love for what you are bringing forth, not from fear or dread.

- Use positive language in your mind, stressing the wonder and joy at this exciting new dimension coming true.

- Picture it as if it has already happened, as if it already exists. Feel like it is already here.

The Opening

Imagine yourself in a beautiful setting on a mountaintop beside a pool of water being filled by a cascading waterfall. The weather is glorious and since this mountaintop oversees the whole world below, you can see forever. Take a few moments to appreciate its grandeur and loveliness. You are surrounded by the blessings of nature at its most glorious and by the power of love. Now slowly zoom down to the world below, counting as you go from twenty down to one. When you arrive, you will enter this new world that you are creating in your vision.

The Story

Begin seeing this new world, new life, yourself, in this fabulous new picture. Watch it unfold in living color! How will it look? Who is there? What is manifesting? How do people get along? Is love part of this new picture? What good things do you see? Note the big picture, but also perhaps some of the details. Place yourself in this future.

Feel the emotions of utter joy, satisfaction, happiness, contentment and peace you are experiencing since the vision has come true. Your emotions are the wave boosters giving your visions impact. A vision must have the concordant emotional element to develop resonance. Think of emotions as the overnight express package to the cosmic post office.

Put your heart and soul and joy into this vision. Stay there awhile enjoying it. Now see your intention carried to the Universe on a giant wave of energy.

The Ending

Just like with every movie, you have the credits at the end. But in this case, the credits go to the Universe. Express your gratitude that the Universe has ALREADY granted this vision. Say thanks for the new world that has already dawned. In a sense it already has — with the creation of your vision. Since there is no "time" in the implicate world and such perfection already exists, you are acknowledging gratitude for something that already is. It's just not yet evident in the "explicate" world. If you equate the Universe to God then this is your chance to express your appreciation to the divine.

EXPECTATION AND TRUST

An important step in the process is to let go of any preconceived notion of *how* your intention will manifest. You have generated energy that will ultimately be in your best interest. Whether it's the exact vision you conceived, a modified version, a lesson, or person who helps you evolve in this life — something positive will come of it. The Universe will manifest what is in your and the planet's highest good. So create your vision and then let it go on the wings of joyous energy.

Your vision will come to fruition, however, if you expect it. This shows your faith in the Universe, your trust in its love, benevolence and wisdom. Know your vision will be successful because you share that vision with the Universe and you resonate at the same frequency calling it forth.

SEALING IN YOUR ENERGY AND WELL-BEING

To conclude the vision, you may want to make a pledge of some action that will tell the Universe that you are willing to make a personal "real world" commitment, as well as a spiritual one. Now zoom back up to the mountain summit, counting up from one to twenty. Surround yourself and the world with the golden light of wisdom and well-being. Then add a layer of purified white light as a protection. Slowly come back to full sensory awareness and pat yourself on the back for your good deed. Congratulations! You have Consciously Created, rather than let unconscious creation control your life and the world's fate. Make a commitment to take time regularly to make visioning a priority. The more you do it, the more you will see a change in the world around you.

AWAITING THE SIGNS

Now that you have dispatched your vision into the Universe, be alert to synchronicities, information that you hear/see/perceive in your mind and other signs that the Universe is offering to guide your future in the fulfillment of your vision. Sometimes people choose to ignore information that doesn't fit their lifestyle, experience or opinions. It bounces up against their resistance to change. But it is in your best interest NOT to exclude anything. The Universe is trying to tell you something, so listen and try to figure out the message. There are many paths to the reality of your vision; you may just not have thought of them all! Be open. Allow in what goodness the Universe has in store for you!

ACTIVITIES THAT INCREASE FREQUENCY

In addition to transforming negative thoughts and emotions through high-frequency positive thinking, there are a number of other wonderful ways to increase your frequency and your resonance with the Universe. These include:

Eating healthy (no sugar, dairy, wheat, limited—if any — meat)

Drinking lots of water and using sea salt, both in their purest natural forms

Meditating

Being quiet in a quiet environment and listening to the Universe speak to you in your mind

Applying essential oils

Body movement—yoga, gentle exercise (Tai Chi or Qigong) or rhythmic dance

Massage

Being in nature

Physical contact with Mother Earth: lying on the grass or on a warm rock, lying in the shade of a tree

Being immersed in water—pool, warm bath, stream, lake, ocean

Getting lots of sleep

Deep rhythmic breathing

Burning incense

Chanting

Listening to high vibration music

Surrounding yourself with high vibration people

Cleansing your body

Feng shui-ing your environment with living plants and crystals

Creating a sacred place in your space

Burning candles with intention

Practicing gratitude, one of the most powerful, uplifting energies

RECEIVING INFORMATION

The meditative techniques noted herein for creating a vision are also excellent tools for opening your receptive channel. Breathe deeply. Put yourself on the mountaintop, in a peaceful natural glade, or other beautiful setting of your choice. Now clear your mind. Gently shoo away thoughts, see them literally depart (going in one ear and out the other.) Raise your vibration rate to match the Universe, knowing that it does. Open your crown *chakra*. Ask a question and stay in repose. Just wait until you see what appears in your mind's eye. The Universe often sends messages coded in symbols so what you perceive may be symbolic of the true message. You may need to interpret it. If you are not sure what you want to ask, request the Universe to give you what it wants you to know at this time. If after a while you are unable to get clarity on any information, don't despair. Perform the act of sealing yourself in goodness (the golden light), followed by the white light of protection. Then go about your business, knowing that your answers will come. The answers may come in other ways than expected or at totally unexpected times. But come, they will!

chapter six

The 'IDEAL' WORLD

I n order for a vision to have great impact globally, it needs to have the unity of many people who share the same dream. While we all come from vastly different backgrounds, races, religions, nationalities and ethnicities, there are some common desires among almost all peoples. In this book, we will seek to create visions that have universal resonance that you can manifest individually or with others.

In order to do that, we should "agree" on some of the general elements that are essential for a world that provides abundance, harmony, balance and peace for everyone on the planet and for the health of the Earth itself. In the following chapter we will create visions that are far more detailed, focusing on specific concepts for transformation around various aspects of life. Let's not worry about how these visions will manifest. That is for the Universe to decide.

The concepts that follow are what we aspire to achieve, but will undoubtedly manifest differently than we can imagine. But in reaching for the stars we'll set an intention that will at the very least move us in the direction we choose to go. We'll be Consciously Creating, rather than allowing the world to manifest by the energies of others who may not have at heart the best interests of the planet and its inhabitants.

"The Ideal World"

- There is peace across the globe. All people are living in harmony, sharing resources, supporting each other and cooperatively making decisions for the betterment of mankind, animal kind and the Earth.

- All leaders are men and women of integrity who put the interests of their constituency before their need or desire for power. Governments act to enhance the lives of their countrymen and women through wise judgment and the balancing of interests.

- There is abundant and healthy food and shelter for all people; every child has an education to at least a high school equivalence and beyond, if desired.

- There is global economic balance, no more Third World and First World countries. Major international debts and trade imbalances are a thing of the past.

- Disease and mental illness have largely been eradicated because we have learned how to manage our energies, we embrace alternative forms of treatment and we have also discovered improved ways to treat diseases and dysfunction naturally. Worldwide healthcare is available for everyone.

- Conscious parents are raising emotionally healthy children who participate in the world with civility, thoughtfulness, kindness and love.

- The world's elderly are cared for by their offspring or their community, so none are alone. There is a loving support system in place.

- All people have values and behaviors that embrace love, respect, consideration, selflessness, trustworthiness, integrity and gratitude. People no longer operate from fear and anger because the new world environment does not generate the need for those emotional responses. People recognize such emotions are unproductive and seldom achieve what they really want.

- Our primary fuel sources are renewable and we have environmentally-friendly technology to operate all our machines, factories, homes and transportation.

- Science is focusing exclusively on creating better ways to live, not destroy life.

○ Global warming has been "tamed" and the Earth's temperature, ozone and weather have balanced out to ensure adequate polar ice caps and predictable, normalized weather patterns and environments supportive of all life on Earth.

○ The ecosystem has returned to balance. Governments, environmentalists and business have found a happy medium that protects animals and the Earth. No longer are any species endangered, and their numbers are regulated by nature.

○ There is clean air and water everywhere and all forms of toxic waste have been cleaned up. Plagues of pests like the bark beetle have been controlled and the Earth is once again a healthy organism. Governments protect natural resources and man respects, reveres and cares for the environment.

○ Everyone has some form of work or play that gives him or her satisfaction and joy, and working conditions that are respectful, remunerative, conducive to creativity and healthy to the human spirit. Even manual laborers earn a living wage.

○ Business has reversed its priority and made workers the top commitment, with the bottom line and shareholders the second priority. Workers see the return of pensions and health care. Corporate executives forego unjustifiably huge salaries and adhere to ethical business practices.

○ Women have the complete right to make choices about their own lives — how they want to dress, who they meet, whether they want to work, if they want to stay home with children or go into the workforce. There is universal day care for those who need or desire it.

○ Men and women have learned how to live as equals and to communicate in a way that unites instead of divides.

○ Human rights are respected and protected in every country and every community.

○ There is religious tolerance everywhere. People accept there are many paths to the divine and no <u>one</u> way is the <u>only</u> way, including the option of a purely spiritual path without following an established religion.

○ Crime is minimal and prisons almost empty. Sexual predators are minimal, treated and cured.

° People are in touch with the knowledge of the Universe and living their lives in harmony with the Universal force and intelligence.

These concepts then will form the core of our initial vision. Those visions that follow will address these and other desires on a more expanded level.

VISIONS *for* A BETTER FUTURE

These visions are only guidelines for Consciously Creating the future. While they encompass a wide-ranging viewpoint, they are by no means comprehensive. However, they do provide a place to begin developing coherence with other Conscious Creators. Feel free to add your own thoughts, edit out portions that do not comply with your views, or develop your own visions from scratch, focusing on issues close to your heart. Use your powerful imagination to create personalized visions for your own life and for the planet.

An important thing to remember is the world is not necessarily going to manifest just as you envision here. But choose these intentions and you give it a nudge in the right direction. Out of the many directions the future could go, you have focused your attention on the ones that are closest to bringing into reality the world of Universal peace and harmony. You are resonating in concert with the Universal symphony, part of a harmonic choir.

You must not become rigid in expecting a particular outcome to come to fruition. Rigidity tends to repel the energy rather than attract it. Just have faith and trust that you've made a contribution creating balance, harmony and goodness on the planet. You will recognize your work when you see it!

VISION FOR THE PLANET

Let's begin our vision on the mountaintop. Close your eyes and feel the sunshine on your face, on your back. In your vision look around and see the beautiful forest behind you, the stunning waterfall beside you flowing into the crystal-clear pool. Hear the sound of the water tumbling into the pool, the sounds of the birds and the rustle of wind through the leaves. You sense the animals in the forest and their benevolent presence. Be quiet for a moment and just appreciate the beauty and the peace.

Notice the gorgeous land spread out below you now. See the verdant green immediately below, the shining city off in the distance, the villages in between. It's time to explore. Begin zooming down slowly as if you were on a magic carpet, counting down from twenty to one until you are at ground level.

As you begin to explore, you see people with happy faces, because the world is filled with a wonderful sense of joy and peace. You now know there is peace across the globe. All people are living in harmony, sharing resources, supporting each other, making cooperative decisions for the betterment of mankind, animal kind and the Earth. In fact the world is moving toward a no-border global One World based on consciousness, not governments, that will eliminate the separation between peoples. There are still individual nations, but these will eventually be merged into a unified entity.

You zoom into a meeting of elected representatives where there is a spirit of true cooperative effort. It is apparent all leaders are men and women of integrity who put the interests of their constituency before their need or desire for power. Administrative bodies act to enhance the lives of everyone through wise judgment and the balancing of interests.

As you go about, you see there is abundant food and shelter for all people. No one is hungry, but no one is obese either, everyone is well fed and healthy. Every child has adequate exercise for body and mind. Each has an education to at least the equivalent of high school. This is as true on one continent as it is on all others.

The global economy is healthy, too. There is global economic balance, no more Third World and First World countries. Major international debts and trade imbalances are a thing of the past. Every nation has found new sources of income in terms of products and services creating jobs for all and increased prosperity across the board. Countries make and exchange goods without the need for protectionism. Borders are no longer hard and fast because the world is starting the unification process in ways that foster economic and social cooperation. Governments work together to solve social, economic, environmental and other problems. The human spirit is honored.

The environment has returned to balance. Global warming has been "tamed" and the Earth's temperature, ozone, and weather have balanced out to ensure adequate polar ice caps and predictable, normalized weather patterns and balanced environments the world over. There is clean air and water everywhere and all sources of toxic waste have been eliminated and residual toxicity cleaned up. Plagues of pests like the bark beetle have been controlled and the Earth is once again a healthy organism. The oceans are no longer polluted, and they support a healthy habitat for sea life and coral. Governments protect natural resources and man respects, reveres and cares for our environment. The ecosystem has returned to balance. Governments, environmentalists and business have found a happy medium that protects animals and the Earth. No longer are any species endangered, and their numbers are regulated primarily by nature and not man. Science is focusing exclusively on creating better ways to live, not destroy life. Our primary sources of fuel are renewable and we have environmentally-friendly technology to operate all our machines, factories, homes and transportation.

Businesses have prospered by reversing priorities. Workers have become the top priority, and the "bottom line" and shareholders, while certainly an important consideration, are now the second priority. Workers see the return of pensions and health care. They are happier and more productive, and the working environment has improved. Everyone has some form of work that gives him or her satisfaction and joy, and working conditions that are respectful, remunerative, conducive to creativity, and healthy to the human spirit. Manual laborers are likewise paid a fair living wage. Farmers are rewarded for feeding the world according to healthy practices, rather than being subjected to the unjust restrictions and profit demands of corporations. Companies have balanced the salary scales so that corporate executives only receive salary and *modest* bonuses after workers are paid adequately. Executives have learned the value of adhering to ethical business practices. Integrity is the hallmark of business in the new world.

There is worldwide healthcare for everyone. Disease and mental illness have largely been eradicated because we have learned how to manage our energies, we have embraced alternative forms of treatment and we have also discovered improved ways to treat diseases and dysfunctions naturally. Miracle cures are a daily event. People get ill less because there is a focus on and dedication to prevention, and we have better ways of diagnosing and restoring health for everyone. Diseases like AIDS, malaria and cancer are now almost unknown. Throughout the world better personal and community hygiene have contributed to the decline of disease.

Human rights are respected and protected in every country and every community. There is religious tolerance everywhere. People accept that there are many paths to the divine and no one way is the only way. All ethnicities and folks with differing religious and spiritual backgrounds get along and cooperate. People everywhere have values and behaviors that embrace love, respect, consideration, selflessness, trustworthiness, integrity and gratitude. Individuals no longer operate from fear and anger because those emotions are irrelevant in this new society, and people recognize such emotions are unproductive and seldom achieve what they really want.

Civility rules people's behaviors. They are polite and considerate to others. Children are spirited and creative, but well mannered and self-disciplined. Conscious parents are raising emotionally healthy children, who participate in the world with thoughtfulness, selflessness, kindness and love. Every home is a haven for its children. The world's elderly are lovingly cared for by their offspring or their community so that none are alone. There is a comprehensive support system in place.

Men and women have learned how to live as equals and to communicate in a way that unites instead of divides. There is true honesty and fidelity in relationships. Men have embraced their kind and nurturing side, as well as their physical strength. Women honor themselves, as well as their families. Women have the complete right to make choices about their own lives and health — how they want to dress, who they meet, whether they want to work, if they want to stay home with children or go into the workforce. There is universal day care for those who need or desire it.

Cities are livable. The population growth has slowed down so that there is a balance between rural and urban, human and environment. There is adequate and affordable housing for all. New public transportation systems eliminate much of the need for autos. The air is clean and breathable. Special communities are created to give the previously homeless a sense of belonging and productivity, to treat their needs and provide services so they are valued members of society. This allows many previously homeless to be integrated back into general society. Crime is minimal and prisons almost empty. Sexual predators are rare and treated and cured. There are enough police and fire fighters to handle all emergencies in minutes. Urban parks are part of the landscape everywhere. Trees are making a comeback in the city. Children play and enjoy the outdoors with their families. People work together to preserve the heritage of old buildings while continuing to blend them with the new architecturally relevant, human-scale buildings that create a welcome, community feeling.

People are in touch with the knowledge of the Universe and living their lives in harmony with the Universal force and intelligence. They act in accordance with their higher consciousness and the power of love that now permeates the planet. Their behavior is routinely guided by that knowledge.

Feel the joy and satisfaction of experiencing this remarkable new version of Earth. Just reflect on the feeling of peace and contentment. Revel in those emotions of being there. Feel it in your emotional center (your solar plexus), feel it in your heart. Thank the Universe now for already granting this world. Feel gratitude for its arrival...for the everyday joy of it. Express your appreciation. Now that you have communicated your emotions, it is time to zoom back up to the mountaintop. Count from one to twenty and allow your magic carpet to return you to the summit. Ready to open your eyes? Raise your lids, knowing you have played a positive and powerful part in the future. Knowing you have begun the transformation.

VISION FOR PEACE

Again, let's begin our vision on the mountaintop. Close your eyes and feel the sunshine on your face, on your back. In your vision, look around and see the beautiful forest behind you, the stunning waterfall beside you flowing into the crystal-clear pool. Hear the sound of the water tumbling into the pool, the sounds of the birds, and the rustle of wind through the leaves. You sense the animals in the forest and their benevolent presence. Be quiet for a moment and just appreciate the beauty and the peace.

Notice the gorgeous land spread out below you now. See the verdant green immediately below, the shining city off in the distance, the villages in between. It's time to experience the new dawn of peace. Begin zooming down slowly as if you were on a magic carpet, counting down from 20 to 1 until you are at ground level.

The first thing you notice is that there is no disturbance in the Universal energy. There are no bombs, missiles or threatening aircraft. There is a blessed stillness in the energetic field. As you zoom over the landscape, you see that all governments have melted down warcraft for use in more constructive ventures, such as the Bible's image of turning swords into ploughshares. Some of it has been converted to peacetime usage. Guns are banned and armies have been decommissioned. Military personnel worldwide may now have an opportunity to join a peace corps-type mission, an environmental protection program, national park patrol, search and rescue, fire protection or programs that provide aid and support to the elderly or disadvantaged young adults.

The world has no more "Hot spots." The Palestinians and Israelis have finally come to accord and the Palestinians have a thriving new economy of their own. Peoples from both countries work and play side-by-side. The light of cooperation, conciliation, mutual interest and loving kindness quenches the hostility of eons. Cooler minds have prevailed and the hotheads have now melted away into the fabric of a functioning new country. The growing middle class is the dominating factor in Palestinian life.

Throughout the Middle East there is a new sense of brotherhood with the greater world. Fundamentalists have an increasingly smaller influence on life as secular majorities have come forward, and there is balance and power-sharing. Most Middle East countries have reached out to the West in friendship and vice versa. The Iranians have agreed to participate in the global disarmament and elimination of nuclear weapons, as have the North Koreans. Al Quaeda has laid down its guns in both Afghanistan and Iraq, and the terrorist group has agreed to peaceful disarmament in exchange for its members partaking in the building up of those nations.

Sunnis, Shiites and Kurds have created autonomous regions in Iraq with all of them peacefully sharing in the oil bounty. The country is healing the anger and madness of the last fifty years as organizations peopled by participants from each sector rebuild the country. America has chosen to withdraw its troops and return home, using those soldiers in productive peacetime programs.

African nations finally are reaping the benefits of elective, inclusive governments. Former enemy warlords and ethnic leaders are now working side-by-side to build up their countries and pull them out of poverty. Corruption is being flushed out. Strongman governments have toppled one by one, leaving the way open for new, democratic and equitable leadership. Governments that have employed any kind of ethnic cleansing have been forced out by international pressure and economic instability. Refugees have returned home in peace, aided by the world community to rebuild their lives. Peoples of differing ethnic and religious origins are finding ways to trade with each other, govern together and live peaceably side-by-side.

People of different cultures worldwide are embracing and learning to appreciate each other to their mutual benefit. Their children are learning in the same schools, people are intermarrying, there are innumerable cross-cultural exchanges. Most importantly, people are working to communicate in a spiritual and levelheaded way that honors the dignity of the other party. Government, religious and ethnic leaders are indeed seeing that their best interests are served by finding common ground with everyone in the picture — internally and externally.

Above and beyond common sense, an abiding sense of love is blanketing the world. People are embracing their former enemies, recognizing them as a part of themselves. Care and concern for one's fellow man is taking hold as the world's guiding principle. Peace is no longer a concept; it is a reality.

Feel the joy and satisfaction of experiencing this remarkably peaceful Earth. Just reflect on the feeling of peace and contentment. Revel in those emotions of sharing the planet in total peace. Feel it in your emotional center, feel it in your heart. Thank the Universe now for already granting this world. Feel gratitude for its arrival…for the everyday joy of it. Express your appreciation. Now that you have communicated your emotions, it is time to zoom back up to the mountaintop. Count from one to twenty and allow your magic carpet to return you to the summit. Ready to open your eyes? Raise your lids, knowing that you have played a positive and powerful part in the future. Knowing that you have begun the transformation.

VISION FOR AN ABUNDANT WORLD

Let's begin our vision on the mountaintop. Close your eyes and feel the sunshine on your face, on your back. In your vision, look around and see the beautiful forest behind you, the stunning waterfall beside you flowing into the crystal-clear pool. Hear the sound of the water tumbling into the pool, the sounds of the birds, and the rustle of wind through the leaves. You sense the animals in the forest and their benevolent presence. Be quiet for a moment and just appreciate the beauty and the peace.

Notice the gorgeous land spread out below you now. See the verdant green immediately below, the shining city off in the distance, the villages in between. It's time to look closely at the growing world abundance today. Begin zooming down slowly as if you were on a magic carpet, counting down from twenty to one until you are at ground level.

We begin our journey in America where we see new opportunities for jobs in urban sectors, giving the chronically underemployed the chance to regain their dignity and to better feed and clothe their families. African-American, Latino and other ethnic or immigrant populations are flourishing. Youngsters are staying in school and going on to college, coming home with ways to improve their communities rather than leave them. People are finding stores and services, previously not available in lower income neighborhoods, finally arriving. Corporate America decides urban America is a good financial investment and locates new businesses in urban areas to train this workforce.

New forms of work are being created through technology requiring limited education and training, and are a great way into a stable lifestyle. Children are growing up to understand the value of a good work ethic and the abundance it can bring.

In rural America, isolation is giving way to connection. Youngsters are being connected to the world through the Internet and through education. They are growing up with new avenues of income for them at home and elsewhere. Small town communities are finding ways to revitalize their economies and recover their downtowns, turning them into living spaces, unique boutique businesses and other ways to create a magnet for the region. Farmers are once again finding good markets for their products at substantial profit. Toxic pesticides/fungicides and chemical fertilizers are a thing of the past. Food is once again healthy and is now being distributed locally and strategically around the world.

Middle-class Americans have been able to ease up on the belt-tightening. Money is flowing and they can pay all their bills and have enough left over for plenty of fun. Two-income families are now optional rather than necessary for survival of the family, and more mothers have the option of actively raising their children. Subsidized healthcare programs and college tuition programs are making life easier. However, people have learned not to over-extend themselves and thus they are able to stay out of debt. Taxes are moderate, and used for peacetime purposes, enabling the growth of personal savings. There is great optimism that money and resources will continue to be abundant so that the middle-class American can live a comfortable lifestyle and the lower economic classes can also move up on the ladder.

In Central and South America, economies are growing with small home-based businesses, regional employers, national companies and international ventures all contributing to growth. As jobs become available, the masses move from shanty towns, village hovels and tiny apartments to better housing, and the lower middle class get a firm foothold on the future. With employment at hand, there won't be a need for border-crossing employment except for those preferring agricultural fieldwork with a balanced pay-for-work arrangement in place. Enlightened leadership replaces the destabilizing factors of governments that subsidized the long-gone drug cartels, which stifled all levels of business. Farmers go back to growing legal crops and getting a good price for them. Elimination of corruption at all levels of government has also put money back into the lawful economy. Information technology begins to open new doors in this part of the world for the middle class.

In Africa with the years of ethnic infighting and strongman robbery behind, the nations get to work building infrastructure and private sector economy, creating jobs. Job training programs become a key to getting people into the work force as international and homegrown businesses begin to populate the landscape. Successful businesses from the more stable African countries like South Africa, Namibia and Kenya start to stretch out into other nations on the continent, as does the arrival of more European, American and other companies. Financial aid comes from international money funds, but this time it really does trickle down to the lowest levels in terms of viable programs. Farming and micro village economy programs now take hold and begin generating ongoing income. Villages prosper in old and new ways, including producing handicrafts that generate true monetary value for the artist's effort. The growth of AIDS has been curtailed, and with robust prevention programs and new affordable drugs to treat the victims, many will be able to live productive lives. Nationalist mining ventures will be started, paying workers a reasonable wage, providing humane conditions, and will be supervised by objective sources ensuring the profits enrich all of the nation's inhabitants.

In Europe as borders blur, all of the nations are benefiting from the increased cooperation, trade and exchange. East Germany will finally toss off the residue of fifty years under Communism and begin to grow again economically so that it becomes a full financial partner with the Western sector. Other former Eastern Bloc countries are flourishing with a mix of small business, banking and new technology industries. With the growth in the European economy, the sometimes-onerous European and Scandinavian taxes ease up, which throws more money into the mix. The underemployed sectors in urban areas start to hum with viable new ways to bring the disaffected or thriving underground economy into the mainstream. Russia finds ways to spread more of the wealth, curbing corruption, mafia barons and oligarchs, so that there is more money in the economy for the average person. With crime under control, international investment picks up. The government begins programs to encourage business at the grassroots level in towns and cities outside of the major metropolises. The old are given enough subsidies to provide adequate food and shelter through their final years and they find social interaction in their local communities. A healthy and growing middle-class replaces poverty throughout the continent.

In Asia, North Korea opens up to the world and the entire Asian region is awash in trade and economic exchange. Chinese farmers are once again busy providing food for themselves and other regions and getting good prices. The communities in the interior are developing new revenue sources. The success of the Chinese economic engine is spreading out to benefit not only the country's own citizens of all stratum, but those in neighboring regions. At the same time the intense disregard for the environment that was a hallmark of Chinese economic growth is addressed and corrected. Southeast Asia, Indonesia, Malaysia, the Philippines — all of these regions see a boom that brings prosperity to the poor and middle classes.

In India the caste system has been eliminated and no longer holds back a person's advancement in life. It has become a thing of the past, all sectors of society are honored, and young people go into the work force from the most remote locations. Villages see renewal through the blending of ancient and modern industries and businesses. All areas protect their environment in support of their economic growth. With vast land and a populace of millions, the country becomes a place that beckons to multinationals looking to expand where there is an eager labor force.

In the Middle East, a peacetime economy enables all of the countries to actuate stabilized economies with money previously spent on defense now earmarked for investment in each respective country. Oil funds are once again flowing, but down to those in lower income levels, and not just to rich ruling families. Each country's natural resources are treated as national, not corporate, assets. Trade is flourishing between the Middle East and the West. Lebanon and Iraq are in a re-building boom. Syria and Iran have embraced the democratic world. The Arabs and the Israelis are developing joint ventures. The poor are participating in the brisk rise in the economy — everywhere from villages to cities.

Feel the joy and satisfaction of knowing there is abundance everywhere in the world, and that you are part of creating it. Just reflect on the feeling of peace and contentment. Revel in those emotions of being there. Feel it in your emotional center, feel it in your heart. Thank the Universe now for already granting this amazing abundance everywhere. Feel gratitude for its arrival…for the everyday joy of it. Express your appreciation. Now you have communicated your emotions, it is time to zoom back up to the mountaintop. Count from one to twenty and allow your magic carpet to return you to the summit. Ready to open your eyes? Raise your lids, knowing that you have played a positive and powerful part in the future. Knowing that you have begun the transformation.

VISION FOR LEADERSHIP

Let's begin our vision on the mountaintop. Close your eyes and feel the sunshine on your face, on your back. In your vision look around and see the beautiful forest behind you, the stunning waterfall beside you flowing into the crystal-clear pool. Hear the sound of the water tumbling into the pool, the sounds of the birds and the rustle of wind through the leaves. You sense the animals in the forest and their benevolent presence. Be quiet for a moment and just appreciate the beauty and the peace.

Notice the gorgeous land spread out below you now. See the verdant green immediately below, the shining city off in the distance, the villages in between. It's time to survey the world's leadership today. Begin zooming down slowly as if you were on a magic carpet, counting down from twenty to one until you are at ground level.

As we take a reconnaissance of world leadership we are aware there is a far greater closeness between nations than ever before. Because new leaders have come to the fore with a true desire to bring peace, prosperity and love to the world and to their citizens, there's been a merging of interests. Borders are open. People identify themselves as global citizens, not just national citizens, because their leaders have set the tone for unity. This presages the time when it will be One World.

The current leaders are men and women of integrity. In fact, there are many more women leaders than in the past, providing balance to the leadership pool. These women bring a collaborative view, rather than a hierarchical view to national and regional administration. There are no politicians anymore. Leaders must demonstrate their commitment to the citizenry through their deeds, not rhetoric. These elected officials are people who have come from all walks of life — various income levels, backgrounds, ethnicities, religions, sexual orientation and education. They may once have been teachers, business people, government servants or wealthy millionaires. They all share, however, a commitment to make life better for their constituency, to plan a future that provides not only basic needs, but enables a good quality of life for all — with art, beauty and leisure time incorporated.

This worldwide group of leaders fosters tolerance and understanding between peoples of all races, faiths, beliefs and lifestyles. Most significantly, they lead by example. Money and power are not their motivators. They operate from love and vision, not from fear and lack. Their decisions are based on a conscious connection with the Universe and what is right and good. They don't presume to tell people how to lead their lives, but instead they create a climate for their citizens to make wise choices. They govern from their hearts and work hard to make the world a more loving place. Often, they have to make hard decisions, but those decisions are fair — not overly influenced by one party or another, nor because they accept "incentives" from influencers. Lobbyists have been banned around the world. Citizens can place their trust in these leaders knowing they have the best interest of society at heart, and their actions consistently demonstrate this. When they err, they admit their mistakes and move forward by swiftly making amends. You won't find hypocrites among them — professing one philosophy and living another. The world is safe in the hands of these wise leaders. They stand for freedom for all people everywhere.

Our future is secure with leaders that bring light into the world. Just reflect on the feeling of peace and contentment. Revel in those emotions of being there. Feel it in your emotional center, feel it in your heart. Thank the Universe now for already granting these wise, caring, effective leaders. Feel gratitude for their arrival...for the everyday joy of it. Express your appreciation. You have now communicated your emotions. It is time to zoom back up to the mountaintop. Count from one to twenty and allow your magic carpet to return you to the summit. Ready to open your eyes? Raise your lids, knowing you have played a positive and powerful part in the future. Knowing you have begun the transformation.

VISION FOR HEALTH

Let's begin our vision on the mountaintop. Close your eyes and feel the sunshine on your face, on your back. In your vision, look around and see the beautiful forest behind you, the stunning waterfall beside you flowing into the crystal-clear pool. Hear the sound of the water tumbling into the pool, the sounds of the birds, and the rustle of wind through the leaves. You sense the animals in the forest and their benevolent presence. Be quiet for a moment and just appreciate the beauty and the peace.

Notice the gorgeous land spread out below you now. See the verdant green immediately below, the shining city off in the distance, the villages in between. It's time to experience the incredible health of the world's peoples. Begin zooming down slowly as if you were on a magic carpet, counting down from twenty to one until you are at ground level.

Wow! Isn't it great? People are thriving and living into viable old age everywhere. There is high quality of life for all. People are trim and well proportioned for their size. Fast food has now become healthy food with the advent of healthier lifestyle choices, and that has certainly been a benefit to young and old. People are choosing healthier foods regardless of their culture and background.

Kids are once again outside playing sports, exercising, riding bikes. Adults are doing everything from rigorous exercise to more cerebral physical activities like Tai Chi. Seniors are doing water aerobics, walking or hiking around their homes. They might even be doing skydiving or bungy jumping because mature people in this world see few limits to their capabilities and desires.

There is an absence of serious disease almost everywhere. AIDS, cancer, malaria — all of the world's plagues are eradicated. Villages and communities around the world have the resources to conduct cleanups and improve hygiene, giving agents of ill health no quarter. Harmful bacteria and viruses are controlled through natural means without the need for drugs. Gene therapies correct or prevent the development of Alzheimer's, Parkinson's, and the muscular control diseases, among others.

Medical practitioners work side-by-side with healers of all types from "non-traditional" disciplines. Energy workers and auric healers are a large factor in the healing of body and mental dysfunction. Energy management healing has become a respected profession on all continents. Doctors are compassionate and communicative advocates for their patient's health. Love and compassion are an important part of their therapeutic toolbox.

In this new world people experience less stress at home and at work, and they have stress-relieving and stress management programs that further relieve pressure. This also means fewer heart problems and stress-related illnesses. People are accorded a minimum of a month of vacation time annually to allow for complete relaxation.

While disease may be reduced, there will always be accidents and other reasons that people need healthcare. Therefore, the hospitals and emergency rooms are plentiful, affordable, well staffed and well equipped. There are enough beds for anyone who needs one and available specialists to treat whatever the condition requires. Doctors and healers, in fact, collaborate around the world via the Internet and teleconferencing.

All healthcare is covered — office visits, hospital stays and prescriptions. Government-funded healthcare is available for everyone with wealth no longer spent on military activities around the world. Insurance companies are no longer needed. In fact, the healthcare programs fund preventative practices, screenings, vitamins, "alternative" therapies and energy healing.

The pharmaceutical companies now must make their products available at prices the governments deem to be affordable and they can still make a profit! They adhere to the guidance of scientists rather than government or corporate interests, ensuring adherence to the people's health. The companies are compelled to make certain "unprofitable" drugs such as snakebite antidote. These are essential to the health of society, so if they can't make them profitably, the manufacturers are required to find smaller companies that can make a profit with these products and sell to them the patent or license.

New cures for some diseases come from old remedies — plants and herbs that modern medicine overlooked. Farmers around the world are now growing these for nice profits instead of cocaine or opium.

Addictive behaviors are being treated energetically with great success, rather than through harsh substance abuse programs. Drug addiction, alcohol abuse and overeating are dealt with through compassionate outreach, aura healing, behavioral therapy and energy management. Mental illnesses are also being viewed and treated differently based on energy analysis and therapy.

A radiance is around the world as people engage in healthy activities, living long and healthy lives. Just reflect on this with a feeling of peace and contentment. Revel in those emotions of being part of this healthy world. Feel it in your emotional center, feel it in your heart. Thank the Universe now for granting such glowing health to all. Feel gratitude for the arrival of this day. Express your appreciation. Now that you have communicated your emotions, it is time to zoom back up to the mountaintop. Count from one to twenty and allow your magic carpet to return you to the summit. Ready to open your eyes? Raise your lids, knowing that you have played a positive and powerful part in the future. Knowing that you have begun the transformation.

VISION FOR HUMAN RIGHTS

Let's begin our vision on the mountaintop. Close your eyes and feel the sunshine on your face, on your back. In your vision, look around and see the beautiful forest behind you, the stunning waterfall beside you flowing into the crystal-clear pool. Hear the sound of the water tumbling into the pool, the sounds of the birds, and the rustle of wind through the leaves. You sense the animals in the forest and their benevolent presence. Be quiet for a moment and just appreciate the beauty and the peace.

Notice the gorgeous land spread out below you now. See the verdant green immediately below, the shining city off in the distance, the villages in between. It's time to experience the arrival of respect for all humanity. Begin zooming down slowly as if you were on a magic carpet, counting down from twenty to one until you are at ground level.

It may seem demand for equality and civil rights dawned with the 1960s Civil Rights protests on behalf of Black Americans. Actually, the fight for equality and respect has always been a quest in human existence. Whenever one people subjugated another, or whenever one segment of a society held itself above another, there has been strife. But as this new day arrives, we have for the first time manifested a world in which everyone is valued equally and has equal rights and equal opportunities. As we have become one family recognizing the humanity in each other, we have shed the painful history of moral, economic and physical enslavement. That has been replaced with loving compassion and support. We help others to fulfill their hopes, dreams and potential, ensuring that we are a strong, unified species. Routinely, the strong aid the weak.

Racial hatreds and ethnic cleansing have come to an end. Religious prejudice is a thing of the past. There are no political prisoners because people are not persecuted for their beliefs. Gays and lesbians have full rights and are welcomed as part of mainstream life. Women share the same rights as men everywhere in the world and can live a life of their choosing. Immigrants are welcomed in their new countries. The physically and mentally challenged are guided, protected and enabled. As the baby boomers have aged, ageism has also ended.

Freedom of speech, freedom of movement, economic freedom, freedom of the heart, freedom of the conscience exists in every corner of the world. Just reflect on this with a feeling of peace and contentment. Revel in those emotions of being an integral part of this humane and moral world. Feel it in your emotional center, feel it in your heart. Thank the Universe now for granting the dawning of this day. Feel the gratitude. Express your appreciation. Now that you have communicated your emotions, it is time to zoom back up to the mountaintop. Count from one to twenty and allow your magic carpet to return you to the summit. Ready to open your eyes? Raise your lids, knowing that you have played a positive and powerful part in the future. Knowing that you have begun the transformation.

Vision for a Compassionate and Spiritual World

Let's begin our vision on the mountaintop. Close your eyes and feel the sunshine on your face, on your back. In your vision, look around and see the beautiful forest behind you, the stunning waterfall beside you flowing into the crystal-clear pool. Hear the sound of the water tumbling into the pool, the sounds of the birds, and the rustle of wind through the leaves. You sense the animals in the forest and their benevolent presence. Be quiet for a moment and just appreciate the beauty and the peace.

Notice the gorgeous land spread out below you now. See the verdant green immediately below, the shining city off in the distance, the villages in between. It's time to experience the dawning of the New Age, the age of Wisdom and Light. Begin zooming down slowly as if you were on a magic carpet, counting down from twenty to one until you are at ground level.

The first thing you notice is how intuitive you are — and everyone else! People have raised their frequency and they are regularly accessing the Universal storehouse of knowledge and wisdom. Before they make a decision, they seek guidance and then respect the information offered. Regularly accessing this source, they have developed the strength to make difficult decisions when called upon. Since everyone is feeling so connected to the Universe, they also feel connected to every other living thing on the planet. We treat everyone with loving kindness, caring, respect and civility because they are a part of us.

Every animal, too, is part of their essence, so animals are loved and welcomed. Because of this ability to reach across the consciousness divide, there is greater nonverbal, loving communications between animals and humans. We are now aware that everything has dynamic energy — from the rocks to the trees to the water — and these must be treated with regard.

People are conscious of their own energies and how to better manage them. Anger is expressed in appropriate ways and then expelled from the aura before it takes up permanent residence and festers. We release any fears that cloud our judgment and hold us back in the world. Those fears that drive our addictions have been examined, acknowledged and gently released

— leaving us with a new sense of freedom. We forgive those who frustrate, anger and hurt us because forgiveness moves both parties forward toward the light. Our natural state of being is honesty and integrity — to the world and to ourselves.

People rely on their energy bodies to alert them to health problems so they can be treated early before settling in for a long stay in the physical body. As intuitive individuals we have learned how to read other people's energies and how to transmute negative energies into positive ones. We are conscious of our own thoughts and how to deliberately change these to reflect positive thinking and a positive outlook. We have learned to monitor our words so they bring back to us what we truly desire, and they support our own positive self-image. Rather than defend our position in a disagreement, we look to see it through the other person's eyes, creating a compassionate resolution and meeting of the minds. And we elect to neither judge others, nor ourselves.

The impact of so many people feeling their self-love and expressing their own loving feelings into the world is truly transforming. Relationships are built around two people's ability to help each other grow and evolve, not around need and dependency. Trust and honesty are naturally the basis for all relationships with friends, family, lovers, co-workers, and even fleetingly with strangers. It becomes natural to reach out to people, to help people without their even asking. Love and compassion also flow both ways as we have learned how to allow love into our lives without sabotaging it. We accept that we are deserving of love from others.

In this world we are passionate about our work, our play and our causes. Personal passion is what gives our life joy. Rather than focus our attention predominantly on the past and the future, we are living in the moment, relishing every morsel of awareness, every sensory experience, every breath. Being in nature heightens that sense of presence and connection with the Universe, and so we protect and seek out Nature. Therefore, to honor nature and the world around us, we live consciously — conserving, preserving, protecting and enjoying what we have.

We practice daily meditation or some other form of quiet time, listening to our heart and the Universe's messages. Our lifestyles allow for that time. In fact this practice is so honored in this new society that society and employers create space for groups to partake. We ask questions to seek the truth and wisdom that allows our lives to unfold in harmony and joy. We believe in our own power to consciously create and perform this act of grace as we go through our lives each day. We use visions and affirmations to mold the future we want and then surrender the outcome to the Universe. We totally trust the Universe to bring us whatever is in our highest good and we are continually awed by the synchronicities and the ways things manifest before our eyes. Most of all, we are grateful. And we seldom forget to express that gratitude.

What is so exciting is that so many others are experiencing this same awakening. Wherever we go, we encounter compassionate, loving Conscious Creators. Our high-frequency energies are attracting new friends and relationships, people who share our worldview. Wise people who help us grow illuminate our lives. One never has to feel alone because there are always people to help carry the load. Each day we feel more and more at one with the Universe, living amongst those who believe in a world that brings out man's nobility and fosters love and peace.

Just reflect on this with a feeling of peace and contentment. Revel in those emotions of being part of this spiritual and connected world. Feel it in your emotional center, feel it in your heart. Thank the Universe now for granting such wisdom and knowledge. Feel gratitude for the arrival of this day. Express your appreciation. You have now communicated your emotions, it is time to zoom back up to the mountaintop. Count from one to twenty and allow your magic carpet to return you to the summit. Ready to open your eyes? Raise your lids, knowing that you have played a positive and powerful part in the future. Knowing that you have begun the transformation.

VISION FOR CLIMATE BALANCE

Let's begin our vision on the mountaintop. Close your eyes and feel the sunshine on your face, on your back. In your vision, look around and see the beautiful forest behind you, the stunning waterfall beside you flowing into the crystal-clear pool. Hear the sound of the water tumbling into the pool, the sounds of the birds, and the rustle of wind through the leaves. You sense the animals in the forest and their benevolent presence. Be quiet for a moment and just appreciate the beauty and the peace.

Notice the gorgeous land spread out below you now. See the verdant green immediately below, the shining city off in the distance, the villages in between. It's time to view a world that has re-established a healthy climatic balance. Begin zooming down slowly as if you were on a magic carpet, counting down from twenty to one until you are at ground level.

The Earth is breathing a sigh of relief. We all are! The planet's temperature is regulated and the ozone layer returned to full strength. Global warming has given way to a globally normalized climate and returned to relative predictability.

This climate and atmospheric management has come about by the cooperation of all of the world's nations, international governing bodies, environmental organizations, corporations, scientists and citizens all working together to effect creative solutions. Greenhouse gases, industrial air pollution and vehicle emissions are controlled or transformed. Jungle deforestation is halted and recovery measures put in place. Companies found ways of neutralizing their waste, using less fuel and employing alternative energy sources. Public transportation and new clean fuel sources curbed the demand and need for burning fossil fuels. People learned how to make do with a little less in order to preserve energy and natural resources.

Polar ice packs and glaciers around the world are solid once again, or are becoming so. The dust bowls are abloom with crops that are getting abundant rainwater, and the practices that caused millions of tons of precious topsoil to be lost are replaced with practices that work with the environment. Deserts are also making a comeback with new succulents and other plant life, but are receding from areas that became desert through poor agricultural and other practices. With the end of the drought, the world's forests are returning to health again, and the bark beetle and other invasive pests are no longer finding a dried and thirsty host to attack. Wildfires are now small and quickly contained thanks to the ample rainfall. Forestry practices in keeping with the natural cycles of nature have ensured a balance that prevents disasters. With an increase in rainwater, hillsides are seeing their natural flora return, so flooding and mudslides are no longer a problem. Mountain snows and runoff bring fresh spring water to all parched areas globally. The healthy rhythm of the ecosystem has returned.

The massive Category 5 hurricanes are behind us. With the ocean water cooling down, and returning to its normal flow cycles, these storms no longer amass the enormous destructive energy that devastates whole regions. Ocean temperature reduction means a better sea life balance. Weather has once again become more stable and predictable. Coastal regions aren't in imminent danger of being swamped by high tides. People are not sweltering in 100+ degree weather in situations that would normally max out at 75-80 degrees. Killing freezes have given way to cold, but more temperate climes.

Humans finally realize their own negative energies have directly and indirectly fed the massive climactic shift. Taking responsibility for repairing the damage is the only way to preserve life. Accord has come. The willingness to abandon expediency, comfort and profit in exchange for the preservation of the planet was not achieved easily, but it has come to pass thanks to a global awakening of consciousness, awareness and commitment.

Feel the relief and serenity knowing that the Earth's climate is once again in balance and that safeguards are in place for the future. The world's energy body is becoming coherent, and you revel in the emotions of a healed world. Feel it in your emotional center, feel it in your heart. Thank the Universe now for already granting this return to harmony. Feel gratitude for its arrival...for the everyday joy of it. Express your appreciation. Now that you have communicated your emotions, it is time to zoom back up to the mountaintop. Count from one to twenty and allow your magic carpet to return you to the summit. Ready to open your eyes? Raise your lids, knowing that you have played a positive and powerful part in the future. Knowing that you have begun the transformation.

Vision for The Land and its Natural Resources

Let's begin our vision on the mountaintop. Close your eyes and feel the sunshine on your face, on your back. In your vision, look around and see the beautiful forest behind you, the stunning waterfall beside you flowing into the crystal-clear pool. Hear the sound of the water tumbling into the pool, the sounds of the birds, and the rustle of wind through the leaves. You sense the animals in the forest and their benevolent presence. Be quiet for a moment and just appreciate the beauty and the peace.

Notice the gorgeous land spread out below you now. See the verdant green immediately below, the shining city off in the distance, the villages in between. It's time to explore the vistas of the land in repose. Begin zooming down slowly as if you were on a magic carpet, counting down from twenty to one until you are at ground level.

As we zoom around the globe we see mountaintops again white with snow, forests verdant with greenery from healthy rainfall. Forests and jungles around the world are protected from logging and deforestation that endangers their abundance and re-growth. The demand for wood is declining as we have found new ways to build without overusing wood in building and design.

Reservoirs and lakes are back to their former levels, providing water for drinking, recreation and sustainable natural beauty. Rivers flow freely and unpolluted. Beaches are clean of contaminants and debris, leaving them once again a healthy place to play, walk and meditate.

Worldwide, mankind finds ways to dispose of waste through healthful and natural means, beginning with creating less waste. Composting becomes a way of life for communities. Landfills shrink to almost nothing. Recycling becomes a major industry internationally. Areas that were toxic dumps and industrial wastelands are neutralized and transformed. Nuclear wastes are chemically altered so they are now harmless and easy to dispose. The dangers of nuclear power sources are replaced with enhanced technologies in solar, wind, geothermal and other sources. With less demand for fossil fuels, oil drilling is no longer a scar upon the land or a source of pollution. Mining interests also come to agreement with government and citizens groups on ways to conduct their businesses without destroying the environment or disrupting the ecosystem. Mankind, learning that there is also a limited supply of metals, has developed alternative non-polluting materials and established an effective recycling system for existing used metals.

Vast areas in danger of being destroyed by overuse or encroachment by mankind are preserved for future generations. Oversight organizations have created limited use permits so that we may enjoy these areas without contributing to their disappearance. Natural parks the world over have adequate resources and staff for their maintenance, security, supervision and visitor education. More bike and walking trails replace roads in sensitive areas. Preservation is undertaken at all of the globe's most treasured sites that were previously in danger of destruction from mankind, pollution, natural threats or simply age.

Balance has come to the world's flora. Prairies and wetlands are once again flourishing. Areas invaded by non-native plants are restored to their original balance and harmony. Hillsides denuded by fire, mudslide and erosion are springing back to life.

Geologically, the planet has become less restless and destructive. Earthquakes are mild and limited in scope. Volcanoes may explode, but they are infrequent and provide plenty of warning, allowing residents to re-locate. Geologic pressure is released, but more naturally, over long lengths of time and less violently. Thus, tsunamis are also practically unknown.

Natural resources and natural treasures are abundant, loved, protected and enjoyed without exploitation. Man and nature are blending seamlessly into one loving consciousness. Revel in those emotions of being in this healed world. Feel it in your emotional center, feel it in your heart. Thank the Universe now for already granting this return to harmony. Feel gratitude for its arrival…for the everyday joy of it. Express your appreciation. Now that you have communicated your emotions, it is time to zoom back up to the mountaintop. Count from one to twenty and allow your magic carpet to return you to the summit. Ready to open your eyes? Raise your lids, knowing that you have played a positive and powerful part in the future. Knowing that you have begun the transformation.

VISION FOR THE SEAS

Let's begin our vision on the mountaintop. Close your eyes and feel the sunshine on your face, on your back. In your vision, look around and see the beautiful forest behind you, the stunning waterfall beside you flowing into the crystal-clear pool. Hear the sound of the water tumbling into the pool, the sounds of the birds, and the rustle of wind through the leaves. You sense the animals in the forest and their benevolent presence. Be quiet for a moment and just appreciate the beauty and the peace.

Notice the gorgeous land spread out below you now. See the verdant green immediately below, the shining city off in the distance, the villages in between. It's time to explore the seas. Begin zooming down slowly as if you were on a magic carpet, counting down from twenty to one until you are at ground level.

At first you hear the lapping of the waves and the sound of healthy shorebirds calling out. As you come in closer, you see shorelines that are clean of debris with abundant beaches and vibrant fresh water deltas merging into the ocean. The smell is clean and fresh, no longer spoiled by rotting kelp, dead fish or algae overgrowth.

The temperature of the water has lowered back to a more natural level established before global warming. Ocean "dead zones" have been naturally re-injected with oxygen, restoring the life to those underwater regions. In curbing the airborne pollution around the globe, it has also lessened those pollutants making their way into the sea. The acidity of the water has been balanced, since with better pollution control, carbon dioxide is no longer acidifying the water. The increased acids previously created a healthy climate for deadly bacteria and toxic primitive organisms to populate the sea, but these are now subsiding in favor of the original sea life. Jellyfish, which feed on algae, have gone back to reasonable numbers and are no longer taking over whole regions, filtering out sunlight and destroying other organisms.

Ocean pollutants have been stemmed and eliminated. Sewage runoff is no longer allowed into the sea before being completely treated, cleansed and neutralized. The human bacterium that poisoned sea mammals has also been eliminated totally through filtering, treatment and prevention. Chemical fertilizers, including phosphorus, nitrogen and iron are banned for use in crops and lawns since their runoff fed the algae growth. Only natural eco-friendly fertilizers are permitted. Harmful algae is curtailed almost entirely without the chemicals to feed it. Red tide is a thing of the past with its noxious fumes and death to millions of sea creatures. Whereas global warming previously reduced the snow pack, which in turn accelerated river runoff and plankton blooms, the situation has returned to normal. All toxins dumped into the sea are eradicated and controlled. Therefore, all of their agents (algae, gases produced by microbes, chemicals, parasites, viruses and bacteria) no longer cause fish and mammal die-offs, poisonings, seizures, disorientation or birth defects. Dredging of the sea floor promoted the growth of harmful algae. Dredging has been stopped until further safeguards are enacted. A coalition of governments, environmental organizations and businesses develop programs to minimize the use of plastics, recycle them and recover plastic waste at sea. Offshore oil drilling is banned.

Ocean-going vessels worldwide are voluntarily participating in programs that curb waste distribution at sea. Fishing practices have come under one set of international regulations. Having lived through a depleted fishing stock, fisherman are now realizing how imperative it is to be environmentally conscientious. After establishing practices that help depleted populations renew themselves, they are staying within catch limits, embracing ways to decrease the impact of nets, looking for eco-friendly ways to co-exist with a healthy and abundant sea while still making a living. Countries that have in the past used dolphins, porpoises and whales as a food sources, have terminated that practice.

This restored ocean includes healthy coral beds and reefs, recovering beautifully from years of pollution and poisons. Newly revitalized kelp beds provide a vibrant habitat for fish. The water is filled with nutrients that feed and support sea life. There's been an increase of previously endangered fish — tuna, cod, orange roughy, Chilean sea bass, among others — that had seen their numbers decline. All kinds of species that were dwindling in number now thrive, responding to the cumulative measures intended to replace balance in the ocean environment. Shellfish are again prevalent and healthy. Otters are making a comeback with abalone abundant once more.

Look around and see the mammals and other larger creatures restored to their habitats, health, number and natural order — turtles, dolphins, whales, manatees, sea lions, seals and seabirds. Mankind has given them back their future. The seas are once again a habitable and hospitable place for the creatures that call the ocean home.

Smell it, feel the waves wash over you, take in the glory of the sea life in your presence. Imagine seeing this vibrant sea life as you view it as a diver, or even a mer-person who can breath underwater. Revel in those emotions you experience by seeing the glory of this restored and healthy underwater habitat. Feel it in your emotional center, feel it in your heart. Thank the Universe now for already granting this return to harmony. Feel gratitude for its arrival...for the everyday joy of it. Express your appreciation. Now that you have communicated your emotions, it is time to zoom back up to the mountaintop. Count from one to twenty and allow your magic carpet to return you to the summit. Ready to open your eyes? Raise your lids, knowing that you have played a positive and powerful part in the future. Knowing that you have begun the transformation.

VISION FOR ANIMAL KIND

Let's begin our vision on the mountaintop. Close your eyes and feel the sunshine on your face, on your back. In your vision, look around and see the beautiful forest behind you, the stunning waterfall beside you flowing into the crystal-clear pool. Hear the sound of the water tumbling into the pool, the sounds of the birds, and the rustle of wind through the leaves. You sense the animals in the forest and their benevolent presence. Be quiet for a moment and just appreciate the beauty and the peace.

Notice the gorgeous land spread out before you now. See the verdant green immediately below, the shining city off in the distance, the villages in between. It's time to view a world that is haven for animals. Begin zooming down slowly as if you were on a magic carpet, counting down from twenty to one until you are at ground level.

As we scan the horizon we see rising high across the skies great flocks of migrating birds. The Aleutian Canada goose previously on the endangered species list is one of these. Such graceful creatures fly long distances to arrive in their various summer and winter habitats refreshed and renewed, finding abundant food, flora and clean water. The world's wetlands and deltas have been restored to their former vitality and health, creating great nesting grounds for all species that reside there or visit. The health of the winged populace gained strength when natural fertilizer replaced pesticides, removing the toxins preventing healthy reproduction. The proper disposal of Styrofoam snow and other forms of ubiquitous trash is policed vigorously to prevent the items from getting into the windpipes and stomachs of birds, as well as other species. In fact such products have been replaced by more environmentally friendly alternatives.

The U.S. is a leader in demonstrating the effectiveness of the Endangered Species Act to bring back animals from the brink of extinction. Thus, the effort has gone global with all nations around the planet participating with amazing success. Nearly all of the 1,000 species endangered or threatened have made a recovery, including salmon, steelhead trout, grizzly bear, whooping crane, jaguar, bald eagles, gray wolf, American alligator, Sumatran rhino and numerous other less known, but crucial members of the environmental balance. Natural diversity is restored. Regional species in North America seeing a comeback include the Columbia white-tailed deer, peninsular bighorn sheep, little kern golden trout, masked bobwhite quail, black-footed ferret, Florida black bear, Canadian lynx, monarch butterfly and Hawaiian monk seal. Government agencies, communities and individual citizens band together to protect habitat and food sources for all such species and to prevent the devastation of habitat lands in the future. Developers, farmers and other interested parties are now seeking ways to co-exist consciously with nature, preserving the natural environment, while integrating mankind in non-harmful ways.

No new Arctic drilling is permitted, and the animals of the Alaskan tundra are free to roam. All other nations have adopted eco-friendly policies that allow animals to thrive. Generally, natural processes thin animal numbers. If adjustments need to be made, however, to keep the balance, this is done in a humane and sensitive manner, and by accessing the Universal wisdom available to all. On the fringes of the wilderness where farmers, ranchers and other inhabitants must co-exist with wildlife, communities work together to formulate creative new ways that livestock, humans and homes can all be accommodated.

In Africa, the world has pressured the marketplace to boycott animal parts or living animals offered by illegal poachers. With no market, poaching has come to an end. Also with peace at hand, there is less chance that animals will be killed in the crossfire of warring factions. Meanwhile, major global efforts have come together to re-establish healthy populations of all the African wildlife. Hunting for sport is outlawed everywhere. Local villages have "adopted" wildlife habitats to care for them as extended parts of their communities, and the government and international groups pay them to do this as a new source of income. This also acknowledges the work they do for the benefit of all.

Down Under, the unique Australian creatures are abundant and healthy in the countryside, finding ample habitat since encroachment is controlled. Large preserves continue to protect the homeland of the koala, kangaroo, wombat, crocodiles, platypus, Tasmanian devil, wallaby and kookaburra, among others. Likewise, destructive activities on land have altered to allow the precious and unique habitat of the Great Coral Reef to rebound.

Polar animals are making a big comeback. With the health of the polar caps since the easing of global warming, their habitats are recovering. Walrus, seals and sea lions, penguins and all their comrades are thriving and finding abundant food, beginning with the phytoplankton and zooplankton that form the basis of their food chain.

Across the world domesticated animals are treated with kindness, compassion and love, plus accorded healthy living conditions, space to fill their needs and ample food. Spaying and neutering programs have solved the pet overpopulation problem. There are harsh penalties for hurting animals, but as people have become more enlightened, these are seldom necessary. Animals are increasingly integrated into people's lives, but through intuitive communication and human behavioral training, such creatures are well behaved and welcome almost everywhere. Humans and animals are not only good company for each other, but they provide the therapy of love where it is needed — especially with children, the elderly, the infirm and the mentally challenged. Animals heal hearts, and humans provide a haven for animal companions.

Now in your mind, feel yourself holding a wonderfully cuddly little creature, or watch the beauty of a bluebird taking wing. Hear the grandeur of a lion's roar or watch the grace of a gazelle bounding across the grasslands. Revel in those emotions you experience by seeing the wonder of these animals that share our planet. Feel it in your emotional center, feel it in your heart. Thank the Universe now for already granting this return to harmony. Feel gratitude for its arrival…for the everyday joy of it. Express your appreciation. Now that you have communicated your emotions, it is time to zoom back up to the mountaintop. Count from one to twenty and allow your magic carpet to return you to the summit. Ready to open your eyes? Raise your lids, knowing that you have played a positive and powerful part in the future. Knowing that you have begun the transformation.

VISION FOR THE WORLD'S FOOD SUPPLY

Let's begin our vision on the mountaintop. Close your eyes and feel the sunshine on your face, on your back. In your vision, look around and see the beautiful forest behind you, the stunning waterfall beside you flowing into the crystal-clear pool. Hear the sound of the water tumbling into the pool, the sounds of the birds, and the rustle of wind through the leaves. You sense the animals in the forest and their benevolent presence. Be quiet for a moment and just appreciate the beauty and the peace.

Notice the gorgeous land spread out before you now. See the verdant green immediately below, the shining city off in the distance, the villages in between. It's time to view a world that has an abundant supply of food available to all. Begin zooming down slowly as if you were on a magic carpet, counting down from twenty to one until you are at ground level.

Food growing, gathering and distribution is a global effort with one major international organization coordinating the worldwide effort. Local "think tanks" develop creative holistic and environmental solutions regionally. On an international level a huge "seed bank" has been developed that collects, stores and distributes seeds around the world to regions where new crops are grown from seeds that very specifically fit the biology and climate of that region. Other appropriate crops, compatible with new regions, are also introduced in this way, to enhance the diversity of nutrition available to each region.

This major organization has set worldwide standards about how crops are grown, insuring that "cover crops" must be planted alternately with cash crops on a regular basis to ensure the replenishment of the soil. This ensures agricultural land stays fertile for long into the future. One of the ways food supplies began to recover was the reclaiming of land previously spoiled by over-planting or unwise agricultural methods.

Environmental consciousness is now the primary factor in how food is grown or raised. As a result, all petrochemical fertilizers have been replaced with natural means of fertilization, thus preventing the ruin of the microbiology of the soil and the contamination of the water table. Natural methods are also becoming used in pest control. Included are an updated biodynamic approach that harnesses the energy of earth, sun, moon and stars to support and enhance the natural growing process and correct imbalances inviting such pests. Where it seems that one reason insects have ravished certain crops is an energetic imbalance, the manipulation of the plant's and the soil's energy has been found to be a successful means to rid the crop of harmful insects. Farmers are also returning to natural means of pollination, creating healthier foods and a better eco-balance.

The discontinuation of toxic pesticides has allowed the resurgence of honeybee populations, along with other crucial pollinators. Genetically-altered food stuffs are banned because it has been discovered such products may not only be unhealthy for those that eat them, but they do irreparable harm to long-standing, natural products and their bio-environments, as well as irreversible damage to the basic DNA of naturally-occurring plants. The limited resources of topsoil and water are part of an important eco-balancing program designed to eliminate waste.

A major breakthrough has come in the alliance of big agricultural industry and smaller organic and biodynamic farmers. "Big Ag" has been adopting more bio-sensitive means of farming and supporting local farmers in cooperative ventures, rather than putting them out of business. They get together and decide which crops are better suited to a larger or smaller operation, exchange knowledge about healthy agricultural methods, and they share resources in getting produce to market. Parity in payment to farmers has been restored, encouraging what is oftentimes a multi-generational dedication to the art and science of providing food for the world, while living with and protecting the land.

Meat and poultry suppliers are acting with greater consciousness, eliminating feed lots so animals have space to grow and natural foods to eat. The practice of injecting hormones and steroids into animals, as well as feeding them with grains has ended. Humane treatment of food animals is now the practice everywhere. And with this additional health of the animals, they have responded by breeding in exceptional numbers, so the surplus is sold off around the world to encourage new herds everywhere. With the end of global warming, grazing lands have returned to full flower and there is abundant food and water for this growing livestock, which is managed to maintain balance with the land.

On a local level, villages and smaller communities are growing more of their local needs in gardens and small communal farms, therefore not having to ship in as much produce from other locations. The job of community or urban farmer is a growing and respected one. As each community accumulates a surplus, it either sells off the extra produce or uses it to barter with other communities growing different crops. A growing bartering system is springing up around the world, and in fact there's now an Internet site where farmers can find bartering partners in their regions.

Education for rural villagers, regional farmers and the big agricultural combines is undertaken to bring everyone under the same umbrella of conscious growing. Consumers — adults and children — are taught greater awareness of the limited supply, the cost to bring food and water to market and the need for conservation. This knowledge is routinely taught in schools.

In cities, hotels and restaurants are now part of a national food bank. All uneaten food that can be salvaged is provided to regional organizations for dispersal to low-income families or individuals. Appropriate leftover food is composted in order to insure high nutrient soil for more food growth. Increasingly, local restaurants are buying their produce from regional organic farmers, supporting the local agricultural community.

Food is moved around the planet where it is needed regardless of a region's ability to pay. No one is allowed to starve. The international food organization regulates and supports food exchange and payments so that farmers still get their fair share and everyone eats. Heifer International has thrived along with other nonprofit programs providing cows, goats, chickens, sheep and rabbits to rural villages. These groups teach the villagers how to raise, use and market animals and then are encouraged to give the livestock offspring off to other families. There are regular grass roots groups in all communities that aid the procurement and distribution of food, especially to those who would otherwise be in need.

Be joyous in living in a world where hunger is only a memory. Revel in those emotions of knowing how glorious that achievement is. Feel it in your emotional center, feel it in your heart. Thank the Universe now for this incredible cornucopia. Feel gratitude for its arrival…for the everyday joy of it. Express your appreciation. Now that you have communicated your emotions, it is time to zoom back up to the mountaintop. Count one to twenty and allow your magic carpet to return you to the summit. Ready to open your eyes? Raise your lids, knowing that you have played a positive and powerful part in the future. Knowing that you have begun the transformation.

VISION FOR HUMAN HABITAT

Let's begin our vision on the mountaintop. Close your eyes and feel the sunshine on your face, on your back. In your vision, look around and see the beautiful forest behind you, the stunning waterfall beside you flowing into the crystal-clear pool. Hear the sound of the water tumbling into the pool, the sounds of the birds, and the rustle of wind through the leaves. You sense the animals in the forest and their benevolent presence. Be quiet for a moment and just appreciate the beauty and the peace.

Notice the gorgeous land spread out before you now. See the verdant green immediately below, the shining city off in the distance, the villages in between. It's time to view a world that has a home for everyone. Begin zooming down slowly as if you were on a magic carpet, counting down from twenty to one until you are at ground level.

A very exciting milestone is reached! We have managed to provide housing to every person on the globe. This housing includes running water, electricity, indoor plumbing and various means of temperature control to maintain comfort. This is achieved in harmony with the environment. Rural areas see the elimination of waste, swampland and standing water through the installation of sewers. Unusable land is reclaimed and made healthy in villages. Construction of housing and business is undertaken in regions that had previously withered away, attracting residents from the city back to the country. People live now in some habitats created from new eco-friendly materials. Better use of resources at hand, including recycled materials, creates others.

In cities, we have preserved and repurposed old buildings as modern new lofts. Low and moderate-income housing arises on areas discarded in years past by industry and cleaned of any harmful agents. Old neighborhoods are urged back to vitality, tearing down abandoned houses and rebuilding new affordable and attractive units. Slums are taken over by public-private enterprises, bringing the regions back to livability. This ensures lower-income inhabitants that they are still the core of the residents, maintaining their sense of community. In these areas people of all income levels and ethnicities, though, are present to encourage diversity and upward mobility for the underclass. Building up — rather than out — on limited land has created more density, but developers have done this with an eye toward developing urban villages. Architects with vision create structures housing masses of people, but still feel homey, intimate and foster interaction by tenants.

While more people are finding the benefits of some types of communal living, they are doing it by choice. No longer are ten people living in two rooms in dire poverty. Housing has manifested for every family in new and creative ways, and whole neighborhoods are reclaimed from poverty and depression. Boats, reconstructed rail cars and abandoned old churches are all turned into homes. Every structure has a potential second life, and honors its new space with respect for the surrounding environment.

Urban sprawl continues but in more controlled and planned ways mitigating the impact on the environment. With better public transportation people can live further from their jobs, easing the crunch in the city. In fact, whole new mixed-use retail/residential centers are springing up wherever transit stations are located. Still many people are opting for a simpler, quieter life, and so they are leaving the cities and the suburbs to find peaceful contentment in the country.

Senior assisted care and communal residences are available around the world in much greater numbers, many of which are funded with government resources. These residential villages are attractive and appealing to the mature generation and offer an alternative to the isolation of old age. There is active participation by members of local society in offering stimulating interaction for the residents.

There are no longer homeless on the street, but special communities are created to give the chronically homeless a sense of belonging and productivity, to treat their needs and provide services, including: medical, substance-abuse treatment and mental health. These facilities are partly maintained by the residents themselves. Wherever possible, the residents are given the opportunity to retrain in new skills and knowledge, allowing full integration with society as a whole.

In places where children are abandoned or orphaned, there are new live-in schools providing quality shelter, food and clothing. Caring, compassionate teachers and caregivers create a sense of family and home, again with active participation by the local neighborhoods so there is no sense of separateness from human society.

As we move into the future, our global society has put a great emphasis on population control so we can continue to house and feed the world's citizens without placing undue stress on the environment to sustain such populations. There is great contentment in knowing that everyone has a place they can call home, but we must ensure that will be the same for the next generations. Now the norm is adapting the wisdom of The American Indian and similar aborigines who made social decisions with consideration for their impact on seven future generations.

Feel the wonder of sharing the planet with all who now have a home. Revel in those emotions of joy for yourself and everyone else. Feel it in your emotional center, feel it in your heart. Thank the Universe now for already granting this great achievement, accomplished while still preserving the environment. Feel gratitude for the arrival of this day. Express your appreciation. Now that you have communicated your emotions, it is time to zoom back up to the mountaintop. Count from one to twenty and allow your magic carpet to return you to the summit. Ready to open your eyes? Raise your lids, knowing that you have played a positive and powerful part in the future. Knowing that you have begun the transformation.

VISION FOR CITIES

Let's begin our vision on the mountaintop. Close your eyes and feel the sunshine on your face, on your back. In your vision, look around and see the beautiful forest behind you, the stunning waterfall beside you flowing into the crystal-clear pool. Hear the sound of the water tumbling into the pool, the sounds of the birds, and the rustle of wind through the leaves. You sense the animals in the forest and their benevolent presence. Be quiet for a moment and just appreciate the beauty and the peace.

Notice the gorgeous land spread out before you now. See the verdant green immediately below, the shining city off in the distance, the villages in between. It's time to view the cities. Begin zooming down slowly as if you were on a magic carpet, counting down from twenty to one until you are at ground level.

This beautiful city represents all cities around the world. It is a place revealing a nice even pace of graceful and contented living for all of its inhabitants. There is a balanced blend of businesses, homes, recreation and natural elements. There is a city center, but also smaller focal points in the suburban areas so that the working populace is dispersed and can access a variety of environments. Transportation includes subways, buses, people movers and other new modes reducing automotive traffic. All of these operate on alternative renewable forms of energy that sustain clear air. The air is clean and breathable, and there is abundant clear water from natural sources, desalinized water and recycled water. Corporations are finding ways to contribute to the planet's health with creative non-harmful ways to dispose of waste from manufactured products.

People find it easy to get to work and they arrive fresh and alert to start their day with zest. Everybody who can work or desires to work has a rewarding job. There is a reciprocal relationship in businesses. People give their employers their best possible effort with enthusiasm, hard work and creativity, and employers take good care of their employees' needs. Workplaces or government cooperatives provide daycare for staff. Ample opportunity is available for advancement with mentoring, study courses, internships and educational options. Every youngster who wants to attend college can secure an education at a reasonable cost.

There is adequate and affordable housing for all. The housing is attractive, ample in space and inviting. People keep their homes in good condition and take care of the maintenance. They are proud of their residences and partake in the upkeep of their neighborhoods. Beautiful old homes are brought back to their glory days and vintage neighborhoods are revitalized.

The downtown area has made a comeback, with a mix of new structures and repurposed older buildings, new entertainment venues and dining establishments. Downtown is once again a vital hub. The rest of the city sees a replenishment of greenery along the streets, including canopies of trees. There are more places to stroll, more parks and more recreational and natural spaces. Open lots are cleared and made into pocket parks, or turned over to the community for communal gardens until owners have an alternate use for them.

People don't have anything to fear when out walking or driving around town. Crime is almost nonexistent. There are enough police and fire fighters to handle all emergencies in minutes. Public servants, such as teachers, are well paid and appreciated. People of all ethnic backgrounds and both genders populate their ranks, and they receive tremendous support from throughout the community.

Gangs have faded away as young men and women have graduated from high school with marketable skills and found desirable work. Enlightened views in society have finally dried up the market for harmful substances. Life has given these kids more to live for than drugs. The underground society that provided illegal drugs is now obsolete. Young people have ample opportunity for upward mobility based on merit and initiative. But there are also support programs to help those who need a little assistance as they go along in life. Society in general has become more aware of those symptoms and needs.

Schools are equally well equipped throughout the city for all grade levels. There are enough classrooms to afford smaller class sizes and these are kept up and have working temperature controls for comfort. Education blends traditional teaching techniques and curricula with innovation and creativity, drawing on alternative approaches, as well as home schooling when applicable. Poor teachers are weeded out, leaving only the best. Youngsters come to school prepared to learn and listen as their parents have reestablished civility and personal self-discipline as a cornerstone of family life. The educational system is a rewarding one on all levels for students.

The city's abundant libraries, museums, community colleges and other learning opportunities also serve the youth. Children have many places to play in the parks, sports fields and recreational facilities scattered over the region.

There are no longer homeless on the street, but special communities are created to give the homeless a sense of belonging and productivity, to treat their needs and provide services, including: medical, substance-abuse treatment and mental health. These communities house and feed the previously chronically homeless, while providing meaningful work and ample recreation — including gardening, animal care and artistic expression. Some of this effort is self-sustaining as this community sells goods and provides services back to the greater city. However, government, philanthropic and corporate entities are unified to provide financial support. Families of the residents also contribute. All of these combined efforts gradually reduce the homelessness in society.

While the need for healthcare was reduced as people have turned to healthy eating habits and more exercise, there still exists a need for medical treatment facilities. Health care is available for anyone at government expense (though partly paid for by corporations), and there are adequate hospitals, hospital beds, emergency rooms, nurses and doctors. Doctors have embraced not only allopathic medical techniques, but homeopathic and energetic treatments, blending both and determining what is best to help the patient recover. Pharmaceutical manufacturers are selling their products at affordable prices, and they are making some "unprofitable" products simply because they are important for community wellness. The process of research for pharmaceutical drugs, as well as development, evaluation and approval for human use, is under the guidance of ethical scientists and doctors independent of the pharmaceutical companies. Profitability is likewise under enlightened guidance.

Older people are living longer lives and they are healthier. Doctors have discovered gene therapies to prevent Alzheimer's so people are more mentally alert. There are also affordable senior living programs providing a good quality of life as the bodies of older people begin to slow down. There are also great community programs offering interactive opportunities for mature citizens.

People don't hole-up alone, going into their homes at night and hiding out at their computers or their TV sets. Instead, they participate in the community and interact socially. They stroll promenades, ride bikes together along bike paths and visit neighbors. The old sense of neighborhood has returned. People help each other. Individuals contribute their time and energy to improve the lives of those in need. There is leisure time for everyone to have a life away from work. People now work to live and contribute rather than living to work.

While there may be ethnic-oriented neighborhoods, all of these neighborhoods are economically vibrant. These pocket-communities are not so much divided and alienated as they are interactive with each other. They are crime-free enclaves of unique cultures, but assimilation is also creating a diverse multi-ethnic melting pot. Different cultures learn to understand and appreciate each other on a daily basis.

What a wonderful place to live! This is your home. Feel the joy and satisfaction of experiencing your life in this imminently livable city. Just reflect on the feeling of peace and contentment. Revel in those emotions of being there. Feel it in your emotional center, feel it in your heart. Thank the Universe now for already granting this shining city. Feel gratitude for its arrival...for the everyday joy of it. Express your appreciation. Now that you have communicated your emotions, it is time to zoom back up to the mountaintop. Count from one to twenty and allow your magic carpet to return you to the summit. Ready to open your eyes? Raise your lids, knowing that you have played a positive and powerful part in the future. Knowing that you have begun the transformation.

VISION FOR FAMILIES

Let's begin our vision on the mountaintop. Close your eyes and feel the sunshine on your face, on your back. In your vision, look around and see the beautiful forest behind you, the stunning waterfall beside you flowing into the crystal-clear pool. Hear the sound of the water tumbling into the pool, the sounds of the birds, and the rustle of wind through the leaves. You sense the animals in the forest and their benevolent presence. Be quiet for a moment and just appreciate the beauty and the peace.

Notice the gorgeous land spread out before you now. See the verdant green immediately below, the shining city off in the distance, the villages in between. It's time to look at family life. Begin zooming down slowly as if you were on a magic carpet, counting down from twenty to one until you are at ground level.

Where families often were the beginnings of our emotional roadblocks in the past, they are now our greatest source of support. Parents are spiritually aware, equal partners who are loving, effective communicators choosing to share their lives in mutual respect and fidelity. Children arrive into these homes embraced, loved and wanted. Courses on compassionate, holistic, creative, spiritual and disciplined child rearing are taught by wise educators and available free to everyone. The home is a sanctuary for every child where he or she can feel completely safe. Both parents have significant time to contribute to the child-rearing effort and in fact are actively involved in their children's school. The family shares participation in the rituals of after-school sports, the arts and other activities that contribute to a well-rounded human being. Both parents lead by example, setting the tone for a conscious, spiritual and loving environment, as well as outreach to others. Even in homes where parents have split or divorced, these same parameters are existent in both homes, and the parents behave with compassion, fairness and understanding toward each other. Laughter is regular fare in each home.

Parents do not project their ambitions on their children. Instead, they encourage them to be who they are and support them in their endeavors. A conducive environment is created for study, while TV and video games are kept to a minimum and designed to support right consciousness. Family meals are sacred time, and each person is given the confidence to speak up, but in a respectful manner that fosters dialogue. The family plans special times just for parent-child interaction providing meaningful bonding and growth. Parents nurture a child's dreams and independence and provide protection from a distance, but not overprotection. A child is supported emotionally and encouraged to express his or her feelings instead of suppressing them. He/she is taught how to respect and regard others — whether the person is an elder, a peer or an "outsider." Parents teach values — especially to appreciate the inside of a person and not just the exterior beauty. Children grow up valuing themselves, experiencing self-love and parental love in equal abundance.

As children grow, they continue to love and respect their parents even as they begin the separation of identity in the teen years. Open communication is the norm. And parents allow that growth without fearing the loss of their "baby" or trying to hold back the youngster. No issues are taboo, leaving the way open for a two-way dialogue filled with truth and honesty. When kids display intuition, they are encouraged to honor it by the adults. Parents are not afraid to say "no" to unsafe situations, late hours, questionable friends. Mom and dad back up each other — standing together on all issues, presenting a united front. Siblings are encouraged to be supportive of each other, not competitive.

As children grow to adulthood, they maintain a close relationship with parents and other siblings even while away at college or working out of town. They take responsibility for their own actions and do not blame others. These aware and intuitive young people are Conscious Creators and they learn to protect and honor their energy bodies and those of others. They are active in the community and demonstrate the lessons of kindness and compassion taught by their parents. When conflicts arise within the family, members meet individually or in groups to calmly and dispassionately resolve differences. Each tries to see the issue through the other person's eyes. Forgiveness is practiced by both generations, solidifying that love is the underlying bond between them under all circumstances. As these young adults bring new partners into the family, parents do not judge, but instead allow their young people to make their own decisions — whether those are seemingly in their offspring's highest good or not. The family always strives to remain the sanctuary for its members, even as grandchildren begin to appear.

As the parents begin to age, the children do not discard them, since the parents have been an integral and loved participant in their offspring's lives. The kids make time in their lives, no matter how busy, to be with their parents on a regular basis, or to call and check in. Parents are encouraged to celebrate their lives and grow old doing whatever fills their heart with joy. Instead of telling their young ones how it was done in the old days, or lamenting aches and pains, these parents fill their own lives with enough interests to stay vital and active. Again, they lead by example. Time spent together with all the generations is precious and valued. As life winds down for the parents, their offspring work together to create a comfortable, protected and safe environment for the elder generation. When parents pass on, the children gather together to celebrate their parents' lives, re-express their love for each other and disperse the property with compassion, fairness and selflessness.

Know this family has blazed a trail of love on the planet and you have played your part in creating a haven on Earth. Just reflect on the feeling of peace and contentment. Revel in those emotions of being a part of this great family. Feel it in your emotional center, feel it in your heart. Thank the Universe now for already granting the strength of family love and support, and clearing away the debris of harmful previous interactions. Feel gratitude for having a vibrant, healthy family life…for the everyday joy of it. Express your appreciation. Now that you have communicated your emotions, it is time to zoom back up to the mountaintop. Count from one to twenty and allow your magic carpet to return you to the summit. Ready to open your eyes? Raise your lids, knowing that you have played a positive and powerful part in the future. Knowing that you have begun the transformation.

VISION FOR WOMEN

Let's begin our vision on the mountaintop. Close your eyes and feel the sunshine on your face, on your back. In your vision, look around and see the beautiful forest behind you, the stunning waterfall beside you flowing into the crystal-clear pool. Hear the sound of the water tumbling into the pool, the sounds of the birds, and the rustle of wind through the leaves. You sense the animals in the forest and their benevolent presence. Be quiet for a moment and just appreciate the beauty and the peace.

Notice the gorgeous land spread out before you now. See the verdant green immediately below, the shining city off in the distance, the villages in between. It's time to celebrate the life of women. Begin zooming down slowly as if you were on a magic carpet, counting down from twenty to one until you are at ground level.

As you zoom around the planet, you see women smiling everywhere. Women feel their power. If a woman comes from a rural background, she has the courage to go forth in the world, or if she wishes to make a life at home in her village, it is a life that fulfills her — one that has desirable options. Shall I be a teacher? Can I create a home-based business? May I do childcare for others? Can I get a job at a local store? Do I want to stay home with my own children?

Women growing up in a city and the suburban regions are filled with optimism, bursting with fresh ideas. They learn how to benefit from the city and there is little they cannot do! Education is available to all who want to pursue it. There are no barriers placed in a woman's way by self, education, lack of money or vision, or allowing men to hold her back. And since men have achieved a more enlightened view of women, such attitudes are in any case rare. If she desires a goal, she can make it happen, and the resources are there to enable her. Opportunities are abundant. If a woman experiences a setback, she is strong enough and self-confident enough to bounce back with greater wisdom. She harbors no fears of her own inadequacy and seeks no judgment from others. She knows she is protected and loved as a woman created by the Universe to bring light to the Earth.

Women are accorded equality in all professions and given equal pay. There is no glass ceiling and they find themselves supported and helped by mentors of both genders in reaching greater heights. Women are strong and independent, but also loving and able to create warm bonds with men and women. They are the peacemakers, conciliators, and mediators — the balancing force in the office, at home and out in the world. They are rising to local, regional, national and world leadership providing the voice of peace and wisdom in the world, creating harmony. Their gifts are manifesting creative new solutions for the evolution and advancement of the planet. Their voices are heard and honored.

In this world women are honored and revered by families, bosses, boyfriends, lovers and husbands. They make wise choices about their lives based on their own hearts and desires, and they partner with men who allow them to grow and help them evolve. Their relationships reflect their emotional health. Such women know they are personally responsible for their own happiness and come to the relationship not putting expectations on the relationship to provide their joy. Joy comes because both partners feel complete in themselves and share the wonders of the journey together.

If the men they attract turn out not to be in their best interests, they leave without fear or harm. These women do not allow men to diminish them, hurt them or make them feel insufficient. However, they also do not blame their partner if a relationship fails. They acknowledge their part in it and are grateful for whatever they learned from the experience. Oftentimes a relationship ends not because of wrongdoing by one or the other party but recognition that the partners are just not growing in the same direction. In such times these women honor their experience and may even maintain a warm long-time friendship with a former partner.

A woman may create an intimate and fulfilling long-term relationship with a man (or a woman!). If a partner doesn't come along, though, she nonetheless can experience a happy, joyous and rewarding life as a single woman, single mom or part of a close community of friends. In this life you can have as many children as you want when you want them or you may choose not to have children and be just as happy. There are no societal expectations either way. If you choose to, you really can have it all — with a little help from the Universe. A woman creates her desire, her vision and asks the Universe to provide the help she needs to balance family, work and time for herself and voila! It arrives.

A woman's life is filled with enjoyments she chooses to give herself — exercise, reading, education, art, hobbies, travel, children and grandchildren, family activities, cooking, sports and entertainment. Where these options are not abundant, women simply enjoy the society of other women.

Women revel in their role as bringers of new life, nurturers, teachers and missionaries of loving kindness and wisdom to the planet. They embrace their intuition and the interconnection between spirit and the Universe. Their spiritual lives are rich with meaning, ritual, gratitude and trust in the innate goodness of the Universe. They see themselves as loved and protected by the Universe, safe in its embrace.

You are a woman living at this time where you can be who you are, free of outside pressures or expectations. You can do what you desire and share your life with those who bring light to it. Your freedom extends to your inner self where you have released all bonds of fear and welcomed the liberty of love and the knowledge that you are a Conscious Creator.

You are a man who treasures all women, who respects and loves them as fellow humans on this incredible journey called life. You live in this time when women can be truly independent and yet full, equal partners...in love, life and work. You honor them and welcome their wisdom and gentleness as they soften the world's harshness and challenges and bring balance to the planet.

Just reflect on the feeling of peace and contentment. Revel in those emotions of being alive in this time when women are fulfilling the ultimate potential. Feel it in your emotional center, feel it in your heart. Thank the Universe now for allowing this time to come. Feel gratitude for being a woman at this time or being a man having the honor of knowing so many women of grace. Express your appreciation. Now that you have communicated your emotions, it is time to zoom back up to the mountaintop. Count from one to twenty and allow your magic carpet to return you to the summit. Ready to open your eyes? Raise your lids, knowing that you have played a positive and powerful part in the future. Knowing that you have begun the transformation.

VISION FOR MEN

Let's begin our vision on the mountaintop. Close your eyes and feel the sunshine on your face, on your back. In your vision, look around and see the beautiful forest behind you, the stunning waterfall beside you flowing into the crystal-clear pool. Hear the sound of the water tumbling into the pool, the sounds of the birds, and the rustle of wind through the leaves. You sense the animals in the forest and their benevolent presence. Be quiet for a moment and just appreciate the beauty and the peace.

Notice the gorgeous land spread out before you now. See the verdant green immediately below, the shining city off in the distance, the villages in between. It's time to pay tribute to the life of men. Begin zooming down slowly as if you were on a magic carpet, counting down from twenty to one until you are at ground level.

The world is filled with complete men — men who are comfortable in balancing their strength and their emotionally-accessible sides. Take the best traits men are known for — nobility, dependability, analytic ability, initiative, courage, protectiveness — and blend them with intuition, sensitivity and compassion: you have today's man. He is outgoing and competent, willing to listen to others, and perceptive about reading people. He treats everyone he meets with regard and if someone is disappointing him, he offers direction or encouragement, and as a last resort he expresses his concern in a clear, calm and diplomatic manner. This man doesn't bottle up his emotions or let anger overtake his common sense. He communicates effectively his needs, concerns and desires with loved ones, co-workers or anyone else with whom he might interact. In fact, he'll throw a cool blanket over hot heads, making sure that rationality and civility prevail. He leads through his deeds, always taking responsibility for his own actions. He is no longer a slave to his ego, but rather supremely self confident in his core. He never blames his parents for his failures and doesn't need the approval of his father or mother. He has long since resolved any outstanding issues face-to-face with his parents. He dealt with those residual emotions through a conscious energy-managing process, expelling the negative energies. And he has done his best to ensure the resolution was a productive and loving one for all parties.

If he has a wife and children, they are the center of his life, and he makes sure that work does not destroy his home life. He is successful at work, but equally successful at home, creating constructive family time in his schedule. While he fulfills his regular responsibilities at home, there is also time for romance and the little subtleties that keep a marriage or relationship fresh and vital.

His relationships with women are as equals. This man works well with women, whether they are his boss, his colleague or his subordinate. As a lover and partner, he is thoughtful, kind, compassionate and strong, but also able to feel deeply and to express his sadness, sorrow or hurt in ways that are healthy. He is willing to take the time to truly hear what his partner is saying and to respond from his own heart. He takes himself seriously when important matters are at stake, but knows when to laugh and not get bent out of shape over the trivial. And he is able to recognize the difference. Should a relationship come to an end, he will be thankful for what was learned and bare no harsh feelings toward his previous partner. He knows she and he have simply outgrown each other.

In this world men are not expected to solve every problem or to accept the weight of the world on their own. They share the burdens and feel supported by others. They have realistic expectations for themselves and for others. This man isn't afraid to appear weak when asking for help because he knows the courage to ask appropriately for help is anything but weakness. He Consciously Creates situations that bring him the aid he needs and allows him to be successful and happy on all levels.

He keeps himself physically fit through exercise that also helps clear his head. He actively participates in the community, works to contribute to a better global future, and extends himself to help others when the opportunity arises. But he also knows when to give himself quiet time for relaxation, meditation and reflection. Fun is part of the mix, too, with time set aside for enjoyable pursuits and outreach with friends.

Spiritually, he is always monitoring his thoughts and speech to cleanse negative energies and create an attraction of positive energies. He acts as a force for good in the world and is in touch with the Universe to make wise choices, hallmarked by integrity and truth. His actions demonstrate his desire to connect to all of mankind, rather than foster separation. His mind, his spirit and his body are all in concert, enabling him to live a life of freedom and joy.

You are an evolved man living in this time where your wholeness is appreciated, respected and honored. Life brings forth abundance and success because you have cleared the path of debris and baggage and Consciously Created the reality enabling you to be the unique man that you are.

You are a woman living at this time where you are grateful for men of balance and wisdom, who are strong, caring and supportive. It is a blessing to share the Earth with men of strength, integrity and honesty, for whom inner joy and contentment is enough. They do not need to conquer worlds to be self-satisfied, just to know and accept their self. We, as women, honor them and pay tribute.

Now let's reflect on the feeling of peace and contentment that comes from living in this world. Revel in those emotions of being alive in this time when men are in touch with themselves and the Universe, and are fulfilling their ultimate potential. Feel it in your emotional center, feel it in your heart. Thank the Universe now for allowing this time to come. Feel gratitude for being a man at this time and knowing that real power comes from inside. Express your appreciation. Now that you have communicated your emotions, it is time to zoom back up to the mountaintop. Count from one to twenty and allow your magic carpet to return you to the summit. Ready to open your eyes? Raise your lids, knowing that you have played a positive and powerful part in the future. Knowing that you have begun the transformation.

chapter   eight

The RIPPLE EFFECT –
BECOMING *an* "ACTIONARY"

Conscious Creation is more than visioning alone. Each of us has the power to begin making our visions a reality by stepping into the realm of action. Our actions resonate powerfully with the Universe, and begin that "Ripple Effect," reaching far beyond our initial motion or thought. Through our deeds, our personal power is manifest in the immediate world and then felt long into the future.

Whether positive energy actions are small gestures — a smile, a hug, a word of comfort, a helping hand — or vast in scope such as starting a worldwide movement — they begin the process of healing that will manifest a better future. While you may initially think it insignificant, even one small action is meaningful.

So how do you begin the process of becoming an "Actionary?"

BEGIN BY LOOKING AT HOW YOU LIVE YOUR DAILY LIFE:

°   Be conscious of the energy you are allowing within your energy body. Have you swept clear the negative energies of fear, anger and self-hate? Are you vibrating in a state of love, kindness, thoughtfulness, self-regard, cooperation and Universal trust? If you raise your frequency, it will resonate with others and help them raise theirs.

- Are you monitoring your thoughts and words? Have you switched to positive thoughts and words that attract people, actions and things you want to bring into your life, and that create hope, joy and peace in the world around you?

- Are you avoiding films, television shows, video games, newscasts, Web sites and books that are filled with violence? These will all lower your frequency level and undercut your sense of hope for the future. Stay with the media that elevate your spirit and reinforce the beauty around us, within us and before us.

- Are you listening to the Universe, the words of wisdom you hear in your head or perceive in your gut — and acting on them? Are you hearing and seeing the message in much of what the Universe sends your way? Are you allowing yourself to learn from these messages and evolve? As you become wise, your wisdom will light a lamp for others.

- Are you living in a state of joy? Be grateful for every breath and every moment. Remember how rich life is. Stand back and think about all the wonderful things you enjoy most about being you, about living YOUR life. Spend a few minutes every day just experiencing the beauty and joy of the moment. Walking your dog, watching the sunset, enjoying the fire in the fireplace with your loved ones, winning a new account with your coworkers, enjoying words of praise from your boss. When you live in joy, you shower it on others.

BEGIN TO IMPACT THE BEINGS AROUND YOU:

- Flow love. When you want to establish love as the basis for interaction between yourself and any individual or group, flow love from your heart out to others. See the pink light extending from your heart to the object of your intent, surrounding the person or group. Throw out your pink net of love. You can extend your flow to animals and even inanimate objects. Lynn Grabhorn in her book, *Excuse Me. Your Life is Waiting*, suggests flowing love to street signs and anything else that strikes your fancy as a means to elevate your own frequency and mood.

○ Reach out to help someone else. Assist an old couple crossing the street with heavy packages. Take a physically challenged person who is otherwise shut in at home out for a day in the park. Help your best friend reorganize her closet. Volunteer to install rain gutters for the elderly lady next door. Aid your co-worker with her practice exam for the real estate boards. Re-do the hair and makeup of a young woman who cannot see her own beauty. Individual acts of love and kindness are among the MOST powerful because they are heart-to-heart transactions.

○ Change the mood in a room. Walk in with a smile. Greet everyone with warmth. Particularly, concentrate on flowing your joy and love toward those in the room who are lowering the energy level. Bring them up to your level.

○ Set the tone in your office. If your office environment is less than ideal, you have two choices. You can leave, finding another job that brings you joy and satisfaction and has established a rewarding environment that fosters creativity, integrity and cooperation. Or you can seek to change the energetic environment in your existing job. Start by flowing love, integrity and consciousness to your bosses and co-workers. Find ways to use your newfound skills to heal divisions between parties, direct people to more constructive pursuits than gossip and develop greater rapport and teamwork. Bring your smile and caring personality to every meeting and holiday or birthday party. Inspire people with your creativity and acknowledge the creativity and effort of others.

○ Fix family relationships. Begin healing old hurts and breaches. Forgive and forget. There is no need to hold anger or hurt in your aura for their deeds. People make mistakes, are thoughtless and inconsiderate, selfish and even deliberately mean. They do these things out of their own fear and suffering...their sense of lack. Bombard them with love, acceptance, compassion and understanding. Most people will respond first in bewilderment (because they see no logic in you treating them with kindness after what has transpired between you) and then later they often respond in kind, in their own way. You're raising both their frequency and yours. And you are setting a powerful example.

BEGIN TO INFLUENCE YOUR COMMUNITY:

○ Start by picking up trash, cleaning up your neighborhood, getting others to share in a once-a-month community beautification day. Such actions have transformed whole cities or regions.

○ Change one house on a street. "Regentrification" of neighborhoods is the act of taking rundown old homes, repairing them and bringing them back to their former glory. It only takes one family on a street to begin a neighborhood's recovery.

○ Volunteer for community service. There is always a need for volunteers with any nonprofit organization, cause or community improvement organization. Find one resonating with your heart and provide your time, energy and vision. You'll inspire others around you to do the same.

○ Become involved in community government. If you want to see direct change in your community, you can do no better than to actually take part in its governance. Offer to join community committees, boards and outreach groups. Perhaps then let your elected officials know that you wish to be considered for appointments. As you come to know how things work, extend yourself to consider running for office. Use your positive energy skills to build up, not tear down the environment. Build consensus with others using your "love net" and cooperative diplomatic skills.

○ Start your own initiative. Whether it is creating a unique local endeavor such as gathering old dresses for financially challenged youngsters to select formalwear for the prom or starting a business that will employ recent war veterans, your creative leadership can change people's whole lives for the positive. Such deeds should not be underestimated for their extraordinary Universal power and resonance.

○ Stand up for the Underdog. There are many in your community who think they do not have a voice. These are the infirm, the elderly, the poor, the mentally challenged and the homeless. You can make a difference by standing up for an individual or a group to ensure their rights and improve their lives. With your limitless creative consciousness and energy you can effect change on many levels.

BEGIN TO CHANGE THE WORLD:

- Get active in local environmental causes. The Earth needs your positive energy and your activism. Whether it is preservation of our resources, the call for alternative fuel sources, animal protection or climate control, there are numerous opportunities for your voice to be heard and your heart to transform.

- Speak up for causes and issues that are meaningful to you. Write letters to your local newspaper and TV station. Find others who share your views and vision.

- Make sure, however, you speak from a position of building a better future, not tearing down what exists. Use your positive energy to call for the future you want, don't focus on what you don't want. If you focus on what you don't want, you will only attract more of it. Be the magnet that attracts the new vision to come forth into reality.

- Join organizations that are already undertaking transforming the world. Lend your wavelength to others to increase the resonance multifold. Give your vision, intellect, creativity, time, money and support to organizations that are mapping a pathway to a new world.

- Participate in Internet petitions for causes with which you resonate. Many causes and groups using the Internet in this way to disseminate important information are proven to be very effective in creating positive change.

WHAT CAN I DO TODAY?

It is easy to become an "Actionary." You just need to know where to begin. Below are some suggestions on ways that you can make a difference. Joining vision with action is the fastest and most profound way to change the world. Below are some ideas, but don't let these limit your creative instincts. Use your imagination to come up with other unique ways to foster transformation!

RANDOM ACTS OF KINDNESS
- with family
- with friends or neighbors
- with seniors or the disabled
- with a stranger
- with nature
- with self

ADOPT SOMETHING!
- Adopt a village in a Third World country through a non-profit
- Adopt a stretch of highway and keep it clear of trash
- Adopt a high school in a low income region and volunteer to create fun, motivational programs
- Adopt a pet from an animal shelter
- Adopt secretly a co-worker or neighbor in need

MENTOR SOMEBODY
- Mentor somebody you know
- Take a friend's or neighbor's child under your wing
- Become a Big Brother or Big Sister
- Teach reading in a literacy program
- Teach professional skills to young people looking to get into your line of work

BECOME AN ENVIRONMENT SUPPORTER

- Recycle

- Conserve water

- Conserve energy and other resources

- Walk, ride a bike, take a bus, use public transportation or car pool

- Refrain from any activity that endangers the environment

- Raise your awareness of how your daily activities either support or damage Mother Earth and think of ways to either expand or alter your behavior

GET ACTIVE IN YOUR COMMUNITY

- Live responsibly daily in your community

- Help with existing community initiatives

- Go to your city council and propose a new initiative

- Join with others in your neighborhood to make your community a better place

TAKE AN ACTIVE ROLE IN A CAUSE OR ISSUE

- Become knowledgeable about the issues

- Determine where your talents and voice are best applied and then act

- Join a committee or group; attend their meetings

- Volunteer to help in the office and administration

- Participate in peaceful protests, publicity stunts and other organization functions designed to bring attention to the cause

- Help with fund-raising efforts

- Speak about important issues to neighbors and friends to raise awareness

- Participate in programs that directly impact the organization's constituency or cause (the homeless, the physically challenged, the financially disadvantaged, children, those suffering human rights violations, the environment, national parks, preservation of historic buildings, etc.)

- Make a financial contribution

- Start your own organization supporting a cause about which you are passionate

GIVE BACK

- Start your own foundation, nonprofit or organization designed to give back to society

- Help fund scholarships or internships for others

- Select individuals who can use your talents, counsel and wisdom and help them get a leg up in life

- Volunteer with organizations providing services to the needy. For example, if you are a lawyer, provide pro bono legal counsel. If a mechanic, provide services to seniors on a fixed income who need repair to their autos, etc.

BECOME AWARE

- Read a newspaper or website that helps you understand where you can best apply your Conscious Creativity for a better world

- Read a book on a topic that illuminates where you can make a difference

CREATE OR PARTICIPATE IN A VISIONING EXPERIENCE

- Establish time in your day to create a vision and communicate it to the Universe

- Attend a unified visionary event, such as those sponsored by United World Healing

- Participate in a United World Healing event online, or download one that you can enact at a time convenient to you

- Get a group of your friends together to create a vision for a better world

PUT SOME LOVE INTO THE WORLD

- Love someone who doesn't feel loved

- Make a clerk or librarian feel appreciated—someone who normally never feels validated by the people he or she serves

- Send love to someone who lives away from you—a friend, a relative, someone you admire, someone you know who needs a hug

- Forgive someone

- Reach out and love your neighbors, even if they don't love you back at first º   Love an animal—hug your own or send a mental hug to an animal in the wild (the squirrel gathering the acorn, the bird in the tree, the raccoon drinking out of your dog's bowl, the duck in your pool!)

º   Love your co-workers for all they do to help you be effective

º   Love the police and fireman who protect us all daily

º   Love the servicemen and women who risk their lives around the world

º   Love the leaders who belief in the power of peace, instead of the power of war

º   Love a class, group or race of people that you may previously have disregarded

º   Love people who care about our world and endeavor to make it a better place

º   Love people who show us that love is the real truth

WORKING TOGETHER

"In this interconnected universe, every improvement we make in our private world improves the world at large for everyone. We all float on the collective consciousness of mankind so that any increment we add comes back to us. We all add to our common buoyancy by our efforts to benefit life. It is scientific fact that what is good for you is good for me." 1

From *Power vs. Force* by Dr. David Hawkins

"...So you could say, what would happen if we had a billion people all doing the same task, with all of them focusing on the same task? A Random Number Generator, a person, or anything? Would you get a larger effect? And the answer is 'probably,' but the form of intention would have to be extremely coherent in order for it have an impact and the reason is if you imagine that that intention has a wave-like structure. If you have more than two waves they can interfere with each other, destroying each other if they happen to interfere in the wrong way. If you have a billion people thinking the same way, the same time, same manner, I imagine you would end up with a very large effect." [2]

Interview with Dr. Dean Radin in the DVD version of *What The Bleep? Down the Rabbit Hole*

Asked what were among the top three conclusions she drew from researching her book The Field on the physics of consciousness, Lynne McTaggart said that one most definitely was the power of the group.

"That means all of us have to get together, thinking the same good things at the same time."[3]

Interview with Lynne McTaggart, in the DVD version of *What The Bleep? Down the Rabbit Hole*

UNITED WORLD HEALING –
The POWER *of*
UNIFIED THOUGHT

UNITED WORLD HEALING AND ITS MISSION

Bringing the world back to balance, harmony, abundance and peace can only be accomplished as a collective vision. While we each can play an individual part in influencing the collective conscious, the power of unified thought has a greater, faster, more powerfully transforming impact. Gathering together millions of people in shared visions and activism is the charter of United World Healing, an organization that was launched in 2007 for the purpose of Consciously Creating a better future.

The mission of United World Healing is: "To unite people and organizations worldwide in visualizing, creating and actuating a better world — one that protects, respects and reveres mankind, animal kind and the environment. To harness the conscious intent of millions worldwide in a synergistic force that can bring about positive change."

UnitedWorldHealing

THE LOGO

The logo for United World Healing is a nine-pointed star with a heart centered in the middle.

First Triangle — The corners of the first triangle represent the cornerstones of the United World Healing mission:

- Vision — Envisioning the world as we desire it to be. Using conscious thought to influence the future.

- Action/Volunteerism — Giving one's time to activism that supports and develops a better-balanced, abundant and peaceful world for all its inhabitants and fosters a healthy global environment.

- Money/Resources — Donating money, goods, resources that can help change the world — and to further communicate and reach out to people ready for a change in world dynamics.

Second Triangle — The corners of the second triangle represent the three intersecting realms:

- Mankind — From the neighbor next door to the uneducated African woman to the Islamic café manager to the Mexican day worker to the Russian scientist...By caring about and for each other, by restoring civility and respect for life we can transform hate into love, division into unity, hunger and poverty into abundance and education for all.

- Animal kind — All creatures, large and small, share our planet and have been granted a place here for the sake of their contribution to the ecosystem/energy system. We as their custodians and fellow inhabitants can draw upon our vision, wisdom, intellect and compassion to protect and foster their healthy and abundant future.

° The Earth — Daily the headlines reveal the extent of mankind's disastrous stewardship of our planet. We can turn it around with a unity of vision, heart, voice and action.

Third Triangle — The corners of the third triangle represent the three levels of consciousness that are the gateway to a better world:

° Individual Consciousness — Learning to manage our personal thoughts/energies and turn them both inward and outward for the betterment of self, mankind, animal kind and the Earth.

° Collective Consciousness — Joining with others around the world to change the global thinking and to free all of us from beliefs and false premises holding us back from achieving a peaceful, economically abundant and environmentally sensitive world for everyone.

° Global Consciousness — Just as we can poison ourselves with negative energies/negative actions/negative thoughts, we can poison the Earth, a living organism that absorbs the energies humankind emits. Furthermore, the Earth has its own energies and consciousness. We can transform the "negative" energy that is causing catastrophic global destruction and damage by restoring its "bank" of good energy.

The Centered Heart — A symbol for the most powerful energy in the universe — love!

Love has the ability to transform almost any person, situation, being or organization into a force for good and well-being. Love is more than an emotion that we feel. It is an energy we emit/project /infuse into the world around us and those we meet. The goal of United World Healing is to lead and teach people in learning to emit positive high-frequency energies that will fill the Earth's "Energy Bank," transmute poisoning low-frequency energies and clear the path for transformation. And then take that intent into the world through action, as well as vision.

Vision-Ins

Imagine thousands of people sitting in a beautiful, natural, park-like setting, all with their eyes closed, thinking, enjoying, manifesting the same fabulous vision for a world of peace, a world where no one is hungry, a place where mankind, animal kind and the Earth are in balance. On the elevated stage flanked by large viewing screens are charismatic leaders, voicing the images that the participants are envisioning. Just think of all the high-frequency energy released into the Universe by all those unified minds!

Just imagine this same scene now in parks, beaches, canyons, forests, amphitheatres and other gathering places around the world. That is how United World Healing is reaching out to the world's Conscious Creators. These events are called "Vision-Ins." You are invited!

Each Vision-In will address an overall global message, but will also break down the day's or weekend's agenda into visions for specific intentions:

- Visions for better leaders who put the welfare of their constituency before their need for power, authority and ego; proven by their actions, not just their words.

- Visions for change in corporate culture putting the welfare of the worker first before the bottom line.

- Visions injecting love and respect into the hearts of those who have refused to come to the peace table and who perpetrate hate and genocide.

- Visions for governments and business to place the environment/the ecosystem before economic gain and political expediency.

- Visions for the increase in general civility in personal interactions — kindness, politeness, regard for others in our space

- Visions for the healing of those who commit acts of domestic violence.

- Visions for a way to address the issue of the homeless in America.

- Visions for the transformation of future terrorists to peacemakers and their willing disarmament.

- Visions for peace.

○ And so it goes...visions that resonate universally, or specifically in that region of the world. Visions tailored to timely headlines.

○

Look for a schedule of upcoming Vision-Ins on the United World Healing website: **www.UnitedWorldHealing.org**. If you have to miss one having resonance for you, just participate remotely online or download it to envision at a time that's convenient for you. Remember, time doesn't exist in the "implicate world." Anytime you lend your thought power to a vision it counts!

THE VISIONARIES AND ALLIANCES

United World Healing is an organization of visionaries at all levels. Its leadership of committed men and women will create visions for mass participation — in person, over the media and online. However, individual members are also encouraged to create their own visions and bring people together to activate them. People and organizations of common interests are encouraged to participate in United World Healing's Alliances, where millions are called together in a single vision. New visions will be Consciously Created on a daily, weekly or monthly basis.

Alliances include:

○ The Alliance for Just and Wise Leadership/Global Affairs

○ The Alliance for Global Peace

○ The Alliance for Global Economic Abundance and Corporate Leadership

○ The Alliance for Adult and Child Education

○ The Alliance for World & Individual Health

○ The Alliance for Family Interaction and Healing

○ The Alliance for World Food Supply and Distribution

○ The Alliance for Family & Individual Shelter

○ The Alliance for Human Interaction

○ The Alliance for the Welfare of Animalkind

- ° The Alliance for the Welfare of the Sea's Inhabitants
- ° And a host of Environmental Alliances
  - The Alliance for Worldwide Temperature Management
  - The Alliance for the Health of the Seas
  - The Alliance for the Sustainability of Worldwide Treasures — National Parks, Historic Sites, etc.
  - The Alliances for Global Woodlands, Wetlands and Rain Forests
- ° Among others...

Check the website for a current list of alliances or suggest a new one!

ACTIONARIES

Everyone can become an "Actionary" at United World Healing. You can participate in the Vision-Ins in your community, you can volunteer for organizational outreach or you can partake in United World Healing's specific local and global programs for the betterment of the world. Individual Alliances initiate many "Actionary" programs around causes and concerns resonating with that particular group and its individual and organizational members. Check the website for opportunities for your participation in world transformation.

THE WEBSITE

The multi-media United World Healing website is the "heartbeat" of the organization. It is United World Healing's worldwide portal and means of member communication. It enables people who cannot participate in a Vision-In to attend via live video broadcast or mobile tune-in to watch on a time-shifted basis when they can meditate or participate, download to an MP3 player or other mobile device. The site is always evolving and updated daily. To learn more about United World Healing, schedule of Vision-Ins, visionaries, membership, Alliances, opportunities for participation, and more, go to www.UnitedWorldHealing.org

A NEW BEGINNING

From this day forward as a newly initiated Conscious Creator, you are part of an exciting New Beginning. What was before stays in the past, but enriches your present. What you experience now is the joy of the moment and the chrysalis of a wonderful future being shaped by your desire and your intent. Through your vision the world can achieve peace and prosperity for all. With your high-frequency spirit and energy you are transmuting the negative energy of people who live with fear and lack as their primary motivation. You are allowing love and wisdom to tip the scale toward sanity, joy and peace. You have responded to the Universe's call to raise your frequency and be a part of the wave of healing.

As more individuals answer the Universe's call for people of consciousness to come forward, you will find yourself collecting friends, co-workers, lovers, partners and associates operating from the same wavelength. Some may not even understand what is happening to them, but because they are high-frequency flyers naturally living their life in the light, they are responding to the call, unaware of what is calling them or why, but seeking to enhance or activate their latent spirituality, nonetheless. Embrace your fellow "Lightworkers" because they will be your neighbors, partners and guides in this brilliant new world dawning on the planet today.

As a Conscious Creator you are the master of the future you experience. Raise your energy and awareness, meld with the all-knowing, infinite Universe, and reap the love, joy and peace that awaits.

acknowledgements

I have been truly blessed by the Universe in writing this book. I am first and foremost grateful to have been given this mission to deliver the message that we are infinitely powerful beings that can manifest our own futures. I see myself as a person whose purpose in life is now fully unfolding. However, I know that with this book, my role is just beginning, because I have also been given the task of leading the world in its transformation by creating the means to unite people — United World Healing — so that we may bring this new future into the manifest world. I am grateful for having been given the vision, guidance and skills to launch this empowering effort.

This book would not be a reality without the many people who helped me learn to listen to the Universe's messages, to understand how it works, and how I could draw upon its wisdom in my life personally and in the greater world around me. My thanks go to my teachers, healers and guides on this journey: Imara, Christel Hughes, Linda Salvin, Bob Wood, Marcela Cruz, Beverly Segner, Ann Battaglia, Ellin Todd, Jeff Donovan, Lynn Van Metre, Donna Blevins, Marla Frees, Cindy Goldberg, Phyllis Arnold and Stephanie Jourdan, among others.

I also want to acknowledge the authors whose wisdom and insight helped to illuminate my path as I raised my own frequency. These include Lynn Grabhorn, Wayne Dyer, Shakti Gawain, Jerry and Esther Hicks, Eckhart Tolle, Laura Day, Kathy Cordoba, David Hawkins, Barbara Marciniak, Katie Byron, Louise L. Hay, Carolyn Myss, Don Miguel Ruiz and Gary Zukov. Their books have been included in the addendum on Recommended Reading, along with many others.

I only hope that you will find the same joy, renewed passion for life and enthusiasm for the future that I have in trusting the Universe and opening myself to listen to its messages.

Bibliography

FOREWORD

1 *Parade Magazine*, Vanessa Williams' quote

CHAPTER 2

1 Marciniak, Barbara. *Path of Empowerment: New Pleiadian Wisdom for a World in Chaos*. New Oceans Press, 2004

CHAPTER 3

1 Hicks, Esther and Jerry. *Ask and It is Given*. Hay House, 2005

2 Gawain, Shakti. *Path to Transformation: How Healing Ourselves Can Change the World*. New World Library, 2000

3 Grabhorn, Lynn. *Excuse Me Your Life is Waiting*. VA: Hampton Roads Publishing Co., 2000

4 Williamson, Marianne. Marianne Williamson Journal from her website, www.marianne.com July 22, 2006

5 Dyer, Wayne. The Power of Intention. Carlsbad, CA: Hay House Inc. 2004

6 Brennan, Barbara. Hands of Light. New York, NY: Bantam Books, 1988

7 Milanovich, Dr. Norman, & McCune, Dr. Shirley. The Light Shall Set You Free. Scotsdale, AZ: Athena Publishing, 1996

8 Gawain, Shakti. The Path of Transformation. Mill Valley, CA: Nataraj Publishing, 1993

9 Milanovich, Dr. Norman, & McCune, Dr. Shirley. The Light Shall Set You Free. Scotsdale, AZ: Athena Publishing, 1996

CHAPTER 4

1 Gendreau, Geralyn. Healing the Heart of the World. Santa Rosa, CA: Elite Books, 2005

2 Lipton, Dr. Bruce. The Biology of Belief. Santa Rosa, CA: Mountain of Love/Elite Books, 2005

CHAPTER 9

1 Hawkins, David. R: Power vs. Force. Carlsbad, CA: Hay House Inc., 1995

2 DVD version of What The Bleep? Down the Rabbit Hole, Produced by William Arnitz, Betsy Chasse, Mark Vicente, 2004

3 DVD version of What The Bleep? Down the Rabbit Hole, Produced by William Arnitz, Betsy Chasse, Mark Vicente, 2004

Recommended reading

Brennan, Barbara Ann: *Hands of Light*. New York, NY: Bantam Books, 1988

Church, Dawson: *Healing the Heart of the World*. Santa Rosa, CA: Elite Books, 2005

Cordoba, Kathy: *Let Go: Let Miracles Happen*. Boston, MA: Conari Press, 2003

Day, Laura: *Practical Intuition*. New York, NY: Broadway Books, 1996

Day, Laura: *The Circle*. New York, NY: Jeremy P. Tarcher/Putnam, 2001

Dyer, Wayne: *The Power of Intention*. Carlsbad, CA: Hay House Inc.,2004

Emoto, Dr. Masaru: *Messages in Water:* Tokyo, Japan: HADO Publishing, 1999

Gawain, Shakti: *Creative Visualization*. Novato, CA: New World Library, 2002

Gawain, Shakti: *Living in the Light*. Novato, CA: New World Library, 1998

Gawain, Shakti: *The Path of Transformation*. Mill Valley, CA: Nataraj Publishing, 1993

Grabhorn, Lynn: *Excuse Me. Your Life is Waiting*. Charlottesville, VA: Hampton Roads Publishing Co., 2000

Hall, Judy: *The Crystal Bible*. Cincinnati, OH: Walking Stick Press, 2004

Hawkins, David. R: *Power vs. Force*. Carlsbad, CA: Hay House Inc., 1995

Hay, Louise L.: *How You Can Heal Your Life*. Carlsbad, CA: Hay House Inc., 1999

Hendel, Dr. Med. Barbara & Ferreira, Peter: *Water & Salt The Essence of Life*, Natural Resources, 2003

Hicks, Esther and Jerry: *Ask and It is Given*. Carlsbad, CA: Hay House Inc., 2004

Hunt, Valerie V.: *Infinite Mind*. Malibu, CA: Malibu Publishing, 1989

Katie, Byron: *Loving What Is*. New York, NY: Three Rivers Press, 2002

Laszlo, Ervin: *Science and the Akashic Field: An Integral Theory of Everything*. Inner Traditions, 2004

Lipton, Bruce: *The Biology of Belief*. Santa Rose, CA: Mountain of Love/Elite Books, 2005

Marciniak, Barbara: *Path of Empowerment*. Maui, HI: Inner Ocean Publishing, Inc, 2004

Martin, Barbara Y. with Moraitis, Dimitri: *Change Your Aura, Change Your Life*. Sunland, CA: Spiritual Arts Institute, 2000

McLaren, Karla: *Your Aura and Your Chakras, The Owner's Manual*. San Francisco: Weiser Books, 1998

McTaggart, Lynne: *The Field*. New York, NY: Harper Perennial, 2002

Melody: *Love Is In the Earth, A Kaleidoscope of Crystals*. Wheat Ridge, CO: Earth-Love Publishing House, 1995

Milanovich, Norma and McCune, Shirley: *The Light Shall Set You Free*. Scottsdale, AZ: Athena Publishing, 1996

Miller, Carolyn Godschild: *Creating Miracles*. Novato, CA: New World Library, 1995

Myss, Caroline: *Anatomy of the Spirit*. New York, NY: Three Rivers Press, 1996

Myss, Caroline: *Sacred Contracts*. New York, NY: Three Rivers Press, 2002

Pearsall, Paul: *The Heart's Code: Tapping the Wisdom and Power of Our Heart Energy*. New York, NY: Broadway Books, 1998

Radin, Deam: *The Conscious Universe*. New York, NY: HarperEdge, 1997

Ruiz, Don Miguel: *The Four Agreements*. San Rafael, CA: Amber-Allen Publishing, 1997

Ruiz, Don Miguel: *Beyond Fear*. Tulsa, OK: Council Oak Books, 1997

Simmons, Colleen: *Crystal Vibration Ailments*. Ballarat, Victoria, Australia: Crystal Vibrations, 2005

Talbot, Michael: *The Holographic Universe*. New York, NY: Harper Perennial, 1992.

Tannen, Deborah: *You Just Don't Understand*. New York, NY: Ballantine Books, 1990

Tolle, Eckhart: *The Power of Now*. Novato, CA: New World Library, 1999

Tompkins, Peter and Bird, Christopher: *The Secret Life of Plants*. New York, NY: Harper Paperbacks, 1989

Zukav, Gary: *The Seat of the Soul*. New York, NY: Fireside Books, 1989

Zukav, Gary: *The Heart of the Soul*. New York, NY: Simon & Schuster Source, 2001

CHANGING THE WORLD,
ONE PERSON (OR GROUP) AT A TIME!

Jackie Lapin, the author of *The Art of Conscious Creation; How You Can Transform the World*, is available to participate by phone with book clubs and small groups of aspiring Conscious Creators. To book a free one-hour discussion by phone, please email: info@theartofconsciouscreation.com.

If you would like to know more about Conscious Creation, go to: **www.theartofconsciouscreation.com**

ON THE WEBSITE YOU WILL FIND VALUABLE RESOURCES INCLUDING:

- ○ An audio version of the 17 Visions in this book, plus 3 Bonus Visions! Listen to the Visions while meditating and Consciously Creating.

- ○ Jackie Lapin's speaking schedule and telephone workshops on Conscious Creation, Frequency Management and Global Transformation.

- ○ Jackie Lapin's Conscious Creation Blog.

- ○ Subscribe for the free Manifest Messenger, daily tips sent to you by email... with new inspirations for Conscious Creation every day!